QUICK STUDIES B.C.

Job — Song of Songs

DAVID C. COOK PUBLISHING CO.
ELGIN, ILLINOIS—PARIS, ONTARIO

The following authors and editors contributed to this volume:

Greg Farah
Charlotte Goglin
Miriam Mohler
Tim Smith
Randy Southern
Mark Syswerda
Rick Thompson
Jim Townsend, Ph.D.

Quick Studies B.C.
Job—Song of Songs: The Books of Poetry

© 1994 David C. Cook Publishing Co.

Published by David C. Cook Publishing Co.
850 North Grove Ave., Elgin, IL 60120
Cable address: DCCOOK
Designed by Bill Paetzold
Cover illustrations by Mick Coulas
Inside illustrations by Scot Ritchie
Printed in U.S.A.

ISBN: 0-7814-5159-0

JOB

PSALMS

PROVERBS

ECCLESIASTES

SONG OF SONGS

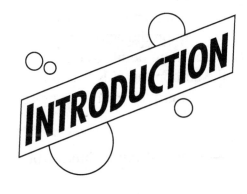

Quick Questions about Quick Studies

We've made *Quick Studies B.C.* as self-explanatory as possible, so you can dive in and start using them right away. But just in case you were wondering . . .

When should I use *Quick Studies B.C.*?

Whenever you want high school or junior high kids to explore the Bible face-to-face and absorb it into their lives. We've kept the openers active and the discussion questions creative, so you can use *Quick Studies B.C.* with confidence in Sunday school, midweek youth Bible study, small groups, even youth group meetings and retreats.

What's so quick about *Quick Studies B.C.*?

They're designed to save you preparation time. The session plans are compact, for quick reading. There aren't a lot of materials to gather, either (you'll need Bibles, pencils and paper, copies of the reproducible sheets, and sometimes a few other items). Yet *Quick Studies B.C.* are *real* Bible studies, with plenty of thought-provoking discussion and life application.

How are these different from other youth Bible studies?

We like to think *Quick Studies B.C.* are . . .

• *Irresistible.* You already know most kids don't jump at the chance to fill in a bunch of blanks in a boring study guide. So we used creative, reproducible sheets and *active* activities to draw kids into Scripture.

• *Involving.* You need discussion *starters*, not discussion *stoppers*. We avoided dull "yes or no" questions and included lots of thought-provokers that should get your group members talking about important issues. And we didn't forget suggested *answers* to most of the tougher questions, which should make things easier for you.

• *Inductive.* Many Bible studies try to force-feed kids a single "aim" and ignore other points Scripture is trying to make. *Quick Studies B.C.* let kids discover a variety of key principles in a passage.

• *Influential.* It's not enough to know what the Bible says. Every session includes a step designed to help kids decide what to do *personally* with vital points from the passage.

When do kids read the passages covered?
That's up to you. If your group is into homework, assign the passages in advance. If not, take time to read the Scripture together after the "Opening Act" step that kicks off each session. There are dozens of ways to read a passage—with volunteers taking turns, or with a narrator and actors "performing" a scene, or with kids underlining points as they read silently, or with you reading as the author and kids listening as the original audience, or with small groups paraphrasing as they read . . .

What if I want to cover more—or less—than a chapter in a session?
Quick Studies B.C. are flexible. Each 45- to 60-minute session covers a chapter of the Old Testament, but you can adjust the speed to fit your group. To cover more than one passage in a session, just pick the points you want to emphasize and drop the activities, questions, and reproducible sheets you don't need. To cover less than a chapter, you may need to add a few questions and spend more time discussing the "So What?" application step in detail.

Do I have to cover a whole Old Testament book?
No. Each session stands alone. Use sessions one at a time if you want to, or mix and match books in any order you choose. No matter how you use them, *Quick Studies B.C.* are likely to help your group see Bible study in a whole new light.

Randy Southern, Series Editor

JOB 1:1–2:10

Testing, Testing

Job, a godly man and a man of great wealth, is held up by God to Satan as an example of an "upright and blameless" man. Satan suggests that Job is godly only because it serves him well materially. So God gives Satan permission to test Job, allowing him to do whatever he likes to Job—short of killing him—to test Job's faith in God. First, Satan destroys Job's livestock—the source of Job's wealth. Next, Satan causes Job's children to be killed. Finally, Satan causes Job to be covered with sores from head to foot. Through it all, however, Job refuses to curse God for his misfortune.

As a group, come up with a description of the worst possible day a high school student could experience. One way to do this would be to have kids form groups of three. Then you could assign one or more one-hour blocks of time (1 p.m.–2 p.m.; 2 p.m.–3 p.m.; etc.) to each group, making sure that all twenty-four hours of the day are covered. After a few minutes, have each group share what it came up with—starting with 6 a.m. and working around the clock. If you have time, let group members vote on which hour was the worst. Afterward, explain that in this session, you're going to look at a man who suffered through a lot more than one day like the one your group members described.

DATE I USED THIS SESSION _____ GROUP I USED IT WITH _____

NOTES FOR NEXT TIME _____

_____

_____

1. What was the worst day you experienced in the past year? What happened? How did you cope with it?

2. Job is described as "the greatest man among all the people of the East" (1:3). Do you think this description reflected his character (1:1) or his possessions (1:2, 3)? Explain.

3. Satan reported that he had come "from roaming through the earth and going back and forth in it" (1:7). How would you respond if someone told you that Satan is still roaming through the earth? Give any support you can for your answer. Point out that the Bible teaches that Satan remains quite active in the world (John 12:31; II Corinthians 4:4; Ephesians 2:2).

4. Do you think Satan's argument to God—that Job was faithful only because God had rewarded him richly for being so—makes any sense (1:9-11)? Why or why not?

5. Do you think it was fair for God to allow Satan to test Job? Why or why not?

6. If you'd been Job, how do you think you would have responded when all of these unexplained tragedies started happening to you, one after another? Explain. Which tragedy do you think would be most difficult to bear? Why?

7. If you knew that exactly one month from today you were going to experience the worst day of your life—and there was nothing you could do to change it—how would you plan for it?

8. How do you think people at your school would respond to you if you were able to deal with your "worst day" like Job did in Job 1:21, 22? Do you think they would be impressed or repulsed? Why?

9. What would it take for you to be able to respond to tragedy, trials, and tribulations in the same way that Job did? Explain.

10. Just for fun: Do you think there's any significance in the fact that Satan's torture of Job involved taking the lives of his children (1:18, 19), but leaving his wife behind (2:9)? Explain.

11. Why do you think Job's wife encouraged Job to "curse God and die" (2:9)? What do you think of Job's response to her (2:10)?

12. Why do you think Job was able to avoid sinning in his response to the tragedies that befell him (2:10)?

(Needed: Chalkboard and chalk or newsprint and marker)

Hand out copies of the reproducible sheet, "Curses or Blessings?" Give group members a few minutes to complete the sheet. When everyone is finished, ask volunteers to share their responses. Point out that although we may not face the major catastrophes that Job suffered through, we all face everyday problems that, to us, *seem* catastrophic. That's when we need to keep our focus on God and thank Him for the things we've been blessed with—including struggles. Even major struggles can help us grow. (See James 1:2, 3.)

Have your group members think of a difficult situation they're currently facing. Write the last sentence of Job 2:10 on the board. Have group members copy it, replacing Job's name with theirs: "In all this, _____ did not sin in what he [or she] said." Then ask: **What would it take for this to be said about you concerning the difficult situation you're currently facing?** Give group members a few minutes to silently consider and pray about their difficult situations.

Curses or Blessings?

Everyone faces difficult situations in life. But not everyone responds to those situations in the same way. Some people view difficult situations as a "curse" from God; others view them as "blessings" in disguise—opportunities to grow and "be stretched" in their faith. For each situation below, indicate whether you would probably view it as a curse or a blessing; then explain your reasoning. Please be honest in your responses.

1. You spend all night cramming for a test (because you didn't pay very close attention in class). After your all-nighter, you drag yourself in at 8:00 in the morning to take the test. You pass—but just barely. Your grade is one of the lowest in the class.

2. A person that you considered to be a friend "stabs you in the back" by stealing your boyfriend or girlfriend.

3. While driving home from school, you get into a small "fender bender." The accident was the other person's fault, but your parents are really upset that you weren't driving more cautiously and "defensively."

4. You've dreamed of playing on the varsity basketball team—and gaining all of the "status" that goes with it. You work hard all summer to make the squad. But on the day of final cuts, you discover that you've been put on the junior varsity team.

5. You are so desperate to go to the prom that you end up going with someone you don't really care for.

6. You decide that it's time for you to get a summer job. All of your friends have jobs at the local amusement park. However, when you apply there, you discover that all of the jobs have been taken. So you have to take a job bagging groceries at a supermarket.

7. You are diagnosed with cancer. The doctor wants you to start chemotherapy and radiation treatment. She explains that all of your hair will fall out and that you'll be sick for a while. Even with the treatment, however, the doctor says that the longest you can expect to live is two years.

JOB 2:11–37:24

With Friends Like These . . .

OVERVIEW

In the midst of Job's suffering, Job's friends come to comfort him. Job and his friends argue about God and the purpose of discipline and suffering. Job and his friends all have a reverence for God, but none are adequately able to speak for Him.

OPENING ACT

Select one group member to be a "victim." Announce that this person is suffering for some reason—perhaps because he or she is in trouble with a parent, a teacher, a coach, a friend, etc. The "victim" must look as sad and depressed as possible during the upcoming activity. Divide the rest of the group members into two teams—the "Comforters" and the "Accusers." The Comforters must come up with comforting remarks to say to the victim; the Accusers must come up with accusations against the victim (suggesting that he or she is responsible for his or her own suffering). The two teams will alternate making their remarks to the victim. The first team to run out of new ideas is the loser. Afterward, say: **"Comforting one another" means different things to different people. Let's see what kind of comfort Job experienced from his friends in his time of need.**

DATE I USED THIS SESSION _____ GROUP I USED IT WITH _____

NOTES FOR NEXT TIME _____

_____

_____

1. Imagine that one of your friends messed up his or her life terribly by doing something very wrong. He or she is now in deep trouble. What are some things you might say to your friend? Do you think it's possible to be angry with your friend, while still showing him or her love? If so, how?

2. What if your friend claimed to be innocent of the wrongdoing? Would you believe him or her? Why or why not? If so, how would you show support for your friend?

3. Divide the following chapters of Job among your group members: 3; 6–7; 9–10; 12–14; 16–17; 19; 21; 23–24; 26–28; 29–31. Give them a few minutes to skim their assigned chapters. **How would you describe Job's attitude toward life? How would you describe Job's attitude toward God? How would you describe Job's attitude toward his friends? What can we learn about Job from the questions he asks?**

4. Do you think it's ever OK to complain or be frustrated about our circumstances in life? Why or why not?

5. Divide the following chapters of Job among your group members: 4–5; 8; 11; 15; 18; 20; 22; 25. Give them a few minutes to skim their assigned chapters. **How would you describe Job's friends' attitude toward God? How would you describe Job's friends' attitude toward sin? How would you describe Job's friends' attitude toward Job?**

6. Have you ever talked with someone who had just experienced some kind of personal crisis like a death in the family, a major accident, a broken relationship, or a divorce? If so, what did you say to the person? How did you feel about talking to him or her? Explain.

7. If you were the one who had just suffered a personal crisis, what would you want someone to say to you? Why?

8. On a scale of one to ten—with one being "not very helpful at all" and ten being "extremely helpful"—how helpful would you say Job's friends were in comforting him? Explain. What *should* they have said or done?

9. Job's friends appear to be offering godly advice for and pronouncements on Job (4:8, 9; 8:2, 3; 11:7; 33:3), but they obviously didn't know the real reason behind Job's suffering. How can we tell which advice and counsel to listen to and which to ignore?

10. One of the main arguments of Job's friends is that God's ways are difficult, if not impossible, to understand. Have you ever felt that way? If so, when? Do you think life would be any easier if God would explain the reasoning behind everything He does? Why or why not? Why is it sometimes hard to trust God?

Distribute copies of the reproducible sheet, "Comforter Evaluation." Give group members a few minutes to complete the sheet. When everyone is finished, ask volunteers to share their responses. As a group, talk through some situations in which people need comfort. What kinds of situations are the most difficult for your group members to address? If no one mentions it, point out that sometimes it's better to say nothing to a person who's hurting—just being there is comfort enough. Close the session in prayer, asking God for the wisdom and sensitivity needed to be wise comforters.

Comforter
EVALUATION✔

When someone else is hurting or grieving, what is the appropriate way to respond to him or her? How can you be a consoling friend to someone while still giving that person as much space as possible? Fill in the following information to see how well you do as a comforter.

✔ *DIAGNOSIS*

There are a lot of things to do—and a lot of things not to do—when another person is hurting. While each situation is unique, what are some general principles you can apply to a future "comforting" situation?

THINGS TO DO	*THINGS NOT TO DO*
1.	1.
2.	2.
3.	3.
4.	4.
5.	5.

✔ *CHECK-UP*

Think of the last situation in which you had an opportunity to comfort another person. Based on the principles you just wrote down, how would you rate yourself as a comforter? Explain.

_____ Great   _____ Pretty Good   _____ Don't Ask

✔ *PRESCRIPTION*

Jot down some ideas of how you might handle that situation differently in the future.

"Who Are You to Question Me?"

After Job and his friends debate God's use of discipline and the reasoning behind suffering, God offers His view. Having heard Job's argument, God decides to challenge Job's understanding. In doing so, God offers one of the most vivid descriptions found in the Bible of the immensity of His power.

(Needed: Question slips, paper bag)

Cut apart the questions on the reproducible sheet, "Go Figure" and place them in a paper bag. Make enough copies of the sheet for each of your kids to have one. Distribute the sheets and give kids a few minutes to jot down some answers. Ask for volunteers to come forward one at a time, draw a question from the bag, and answer it to the best of their ability. Then have the rest of the group vote on whether or not the answer would satisfy five-year-old Cousin Joey. If the answer is deemed "unsatisfactory," ask other kids to offer the answers they came up with for that question. After all of the questions have been answered, explain that in this session, you're going to be looking at tough questions of a different kind.

DATE I USED THIS SESSION _____ GROUP I USED IT WITH _____

NOTES FOR NEXT TIME _____

_____

_____

1. What's the hardest question you've ever been asked? How did you respond? Explain.

2. If you were Job, how do you think you'd react when you heard God's voice? (In addition to being awe-struck and maybe a little frightened, perhaps Job was relieved to hear God's voice—after all, God's silence regarding Job's suffering probably added to Job's suffering.)

3. Why do you think God asks Job so many questions in Job 38–41? (Perhaps God wanted to give Job an eternal perspective. He wanted Job to see that just as God has a purpose for everything that happens in the universe, so He has a purpose for everything that happens in our lives.)

4. God's words in Job 38–41 are a response to Job's questioning in passages like Job 7. In one sentence, how would you sum up God's response to Job? (Perhaps "Who are you to question Me?")

5. Of course, God's "job description" in Job 38–41 lists just a minute percentage of all the things He actually does. But how does just this small sampling of God's work affect your view of Him? Explain.

6. Of the images that God paints detailing examples of His power, which do you find most impressive? Why?

7. If God knows so many details about the animals that He created (Job 39), how much do you think He knows about you? Does it comfort you or intimidate you to know that God knows so much about you? How might that help you the next time you feel alone?

8. If you were Job, how do you think you would answer God's questions (40:1)? Compare group members' responses with Job's response in Job 40:3-5.

9. Are there people today who still question God? Have *you* ever questioned God? If so, how do you think reading Job 38–41 might affect a person's tendency to question?

10. What do you think a person should do when he or she truly does not understand why God would allow something bad to happen to him or her?

(Needed: Chalkboard and chalk or newsprint and marker)

Ask your group members to call out any description or characteristic of God that they can think of. Write group members' responses on the board as they're given. Responses might include things like "all-knowing," "all-powerful," "all-seeing," "loving," "holy," and "merciful." Suggest that when we face trying situations, we tend to forget these aspects of God. Give your group members a minute or two to silently consider some of their questions or frustrations concerning God. Point out that when God responded to Job, He never directly addressed Job's questions. Instead, God questioned Job back. In doing so, God showed Job that He has complete control of everything. Encourage your group members to give their problems and questions to God and simply trust Him during the confusing times of life. Close with a group prayer, giving several group members an opportunity to praise God for who He is.

GoFigure

Your five-year-old cousin Joey is the curious type.
He asked you the questions listed below because he
was certain that you'd have the answers. You'd hate
to disappoint the little tyke, so you need to come up
with a plausible-sounding answer for each question.
Use your creativity.

Where does darkness live during the day?

Where is snow stored?

Where does the TV picture come from?

Where does a tornado come from?

Why do worms come out of the ground after it rains?

If God talks to us, why can't we hear Him?

Where does God live?

Why do people die?

JOB 42

A Fresh Start

After having been rebuked for his questioning, Job humbles himself before God. God then rebukes Job's friends for offering ungodly advice and instructs Job to pray for their forgiveness. The Book of Job ends with God's restoration of Job and His blessing Job with twice as much as Job had previously.

(Needed: Several prizes, boxes)

Ask for three volunteers to compete in a trivia quiz. Give the winner of the contest a prize (perhaps a candy bar). Play several rounds—using different contestants—so that several people receive prizes. Then give all of your prize winners an opportunity to trade their prizes for other, "mystery" prizes—which may or may not be more valuable than their original prizes. (Mystery prizes might include a can of dog food, a $5 gift certificate, a ball of aluminum foil, and a pair of wacky sunglasses.) After several prize winners have either benefited from or been burned by their trades, stop the game. Then ask: **Would you be willing to sacrifice all that Job lost and suffer all that Job suffered if you knew that after a certain amount of time, you would be blessed with twice as much as you had before? Why or why not?** Point out that Job didn't know he would be rewarded after his suffering.

DATE I USED THIS SESSION _____ GROUP I USED IT WITH _____

NOTES FOR NEXT TIME _____

_____

_____

1. Have you ever been in a situation in which you had absolutely no control of the things that were going on around you? If so, what were the circumstances? How did you feel? What did you do?

2. How do you think Job felt as he responded to God after being rebuked for the past four chapters? (Perhaps he was ashamed that he'd ever dared to question God in the first place. We get a vivid sense of Job's attitude in Job 42:6.)

3. Do you think most people you know would agree with Job's statement to God in Job 42:2? Why or why not?

4. True or false: Recognizing that God knows everything makes living life much easier. Support your answer.

5. Job used dust and ashes to demonstrate his repentance (42:6). How do you think Christians today should demonstrate their repentance when they've committed a sin against the Lord?

6. How do you think Job's "wise" counselor friends felt when God rebuked them (42:7)? (In addition to being frightened, perhaps they also came to the realization that they shouldn't pretend to speak for the Lord when they really don't.) **What types of people today pretend to speak for the Lord when offering advice to others? How do you think God deals with such people?**

7. Do you find anything interesting in the fact that God ordered Job's friends to go through Job in repenting of their sin (42:8, 9)? Explain. (Perhaps God was publicly acknowledging Job's godliness.)

8. How do you think Job felt when God blessed him with twice as much as he'd had before (42:10)? Do you think Job felt that his ordeal was "worth it"? Explain.

9. How do you think Job might have felt if the Lord hadn't blessed him so richly after his ordeal? If God had allowed Job to remain in his suffering state until he died, how might Job's attitude toward God have been different? Explain.

10. Imagine "Grandpa Job" with his grandchildren (42:16). **What three lessons do you think Job might try to teach to them based on his experiences? Explain.** (Perhaps that God is always in control, even when circumstances go sour; that we should always remain faithful to God; and that nothing can happen to us that God doesn't allow.)

Hand out copies of the reproducible sheet, "Why Is This Happening?" Let group members work in pairs or small groups to complete the sheet. When everyone is finished, ask volunteers to share what they came up with. Then have the members of each pair or small group pray for each other, asking for God's help in dealing with "unfair" and hard-to-explain situations.

Why Is This Happening?

Like Job, we're sometimes faced with situations that we don't understand. Answer the following questions to determine how you can and should respond to such situations.

1. When I don't understand why something is happening in my life, I'm tempted to . . .
(List four or five different ways in which someone might respond negatively to such a situation.)

2. Based on Job's example, when I don't understand why something is happening in my life, I should . . . (List four or five different ways in which someone might respond positively to such a situation.)

3. Describe an "unfair" situation in your life that you're currently going through or that you've gone through recently.

4. Which of the ideas you listed for question #2 do you think would work best for your current (or recent) "unfair" situation? How can you put that idea into action?

PSALM 1

The Blessed and the Chaff

The Book of Psalms portrays humans' desire to worship and praise the Lord. The Psalms are known for their adaptability to music and their comforting words of wisdom. Psalm 1 describes two paths in the journey of life. One places us in God's favor, with continued happiness and peace. The other leads us to reject God, follow the wrong crowd, and suffer the consequences.

(Needed: Prize [optional])

Hand out paper and pencils. Have each group member complete the following statement: "Happiness is . . ." After a minute or two, collect the papers. Then, one at a time, read the responses aloud. After you read each response, have group members vote on whose response they think it is. Award a point for each person who guesses correctly. At the end of the contest, you might want to give a prize to the person with the most points. Afterward, point out that in this session, you're going to be looking at what the psalmist said about true happiness and a meaningful life.

DATE I USED THIS SESSION _____ GROUP I USED IT WITH _____

NOTES FOR NEXT TIME _____

_____

_____

1. What would you need to have in order to live a truly happy life? Why are those things important to your happiness?

2. Besides knowing that God promises us real contentment when we follow His way (1:1), what are some of His other loving characteristics that you see in Psalm 1? (He directs our thoughts away from evil [1:2]. He wants us to grow and prosper [1:3]. He protects us from our enemies [1:6].)

3. What do you think it means to "walk in the counsel of the wicked," "stand in the way of sinners," and "sit in the seat of mockers" (1:1)? (Hang out or be associated with evil, ungodly people.)

4. What are some ways we can meditate "day and night" on the law of the Lord (1:2)? (Pray silently to God in the middle of a school day; ask the Lord for help during a big exam; remind ourselves that the Lord is with us when we're with our friends; notice God's influence in the world and in your life; memorize a Bible verse and think about it on and off during the day.)

5. Psalm 1:3 tells us that "whatever [a blessed person] does prospers." Does that mean that all Christians will be wealthy and successful? Explain. (Perhaps not in a material sense; but if we follow the guidelines set in Psalm 1:1-3, we will certainly prosper spiritually.)

6. What does Psalm 1:3 mean by yielding "fruit in season?" (Just as a strong apple tree will produce luscious apples when it's time, so will our healthy spiritual condition produce a variety of creative and God-pleasing talents.)

7. Have you ever felt separated from God? If so, how did it feel? What were the circumstances that caused you to feel this way?

8. The "chaff" mentioned in Psalm 1:4 is like the outer skin of a fruit or vegetable—a banana peel, a watermelon rind, a corn husk, etc. Why do you think the psalmist compares the wicked to chaff? (Just as the chaff that the wind blows away is utterly useless, so are the wicked utterly useless to God.)

9. When was the last time you recognized firsthand that "the Lord watches over the way of the righteous" (1:6)?

10. Based on Psalm 1, what are the differences between a "blessed" (1:1) person and a "wicked" (1:4) person?

11. If you had to sum up the principles in Psalm 1 in one sentence, what would you say?

Hand out copies of the reoproducible sheet, "The Tree of Happiness." Let group members work in pairs or small groups to complete the sheet. When everyone is finished, go through the answers as a group. (The correct answers are as follows: [1] Reading God's Word; [2] Thinking about God night and day; [3] Pursuing righteousness; [4] Not mocking others; [5] Following Jesus; [6] Praying; [7] Respecting others; [8] Producing fruit.) Then briefly discuss how each item listed on the sheet can bring true happiness and which of the items are most difficult for your group members. Emphasize the importance of each item in a truly "happy" life.

THE TREE OF HAPPINESS

Unscramble the following words to discover some of the keys to happiness described in Psalm 1.

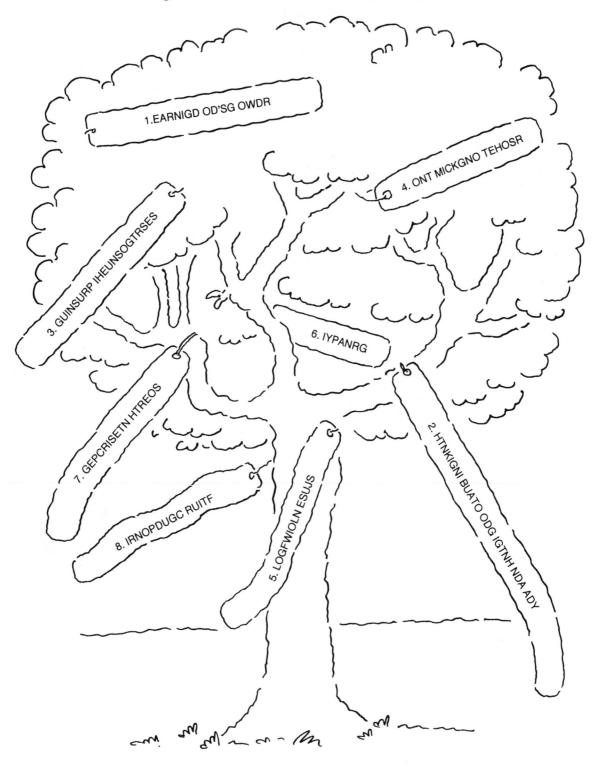

1. EARNIGD OD'SG OWDR

4. ONT MICKGNO TEHOSR

3. GUINSURP IHEUNSOGTRSES

6. IYPANRG

7. GEPCRISETN HTREOS

8. IRNOPDUGC RUITF

5. LOGFWIOLN ESUIS

2. HTNKIGNI BUATO ODG IGTNH NDA ADY

PSALM 4

Sleep in Heavenly Peace

King David writes this psalm in the midst of some kind of calamity—perhaps a drought. He asks God for relief from his distress, then urges the ungodly to turn from their idolatry. David recognizes that the Lord is the ultimate source of joy. Knowing this, he is able to sleep peacefully.

(Needed: Props for the skit [optional])

Ask for seven volunteers to participate in a skit. (If your group is small, you may double up on parts and use fewer volunteers.) Hand a copy of the reproducible sheet, "The Distractions," to each volunteer. Assign roles. Give the actors a minute or two to look over the skit and decide what they're going to do; then have them perform. Afterward, explain that in this session, you'll be looking David's secret for a peaceful night's sleep.

DATE I USED THIS SESSION _____ GROUP I USED IT WITH _____

NOTES FOR NEXT TIME _____

_____

_____

1. Are you a light sleeper or a heavy sleeper? What things most often distract you from getting a good night's sleep? What kinds of things help you get to sleep?

2. David loved to worship God, especially through his music. What is your favorite way of expressing your love to the Lord? (Praying, singing, participating in youth group activities, helping a friend, writing poetry, having devotions, listening to music, working out, playing sports, reading the Bible or Christian books, etc.)

3. It upset David to hear people talk against God and dishonor Him (4:2). In what ways do people today talk against God and dishonor Him? Do these actions upset you as much as they might have upset David? Why or why not?

4. What does it mean to be "set apart" by God (4:3)? Do you ever feel like you're set apart? If so, in what ways? (Some people may feel set apart when they're with Christian friends.)

5. Do you think it's possible to be angry without sinning? Explain. (Anger is an emotion; it's not wrong to feel anger. But acting on your anger in an inappropriate way is wrong.)

6. Give an example of a time when you were angry, but did not sin. Give an example of a time when you allowed your anger to get the best of you.

7. Have you or anyone you know ever been so depressed that you felt like the people described in Psalm 4:6 who asked, "Who can show us any good?"? If so, what were the circumstances? What happened?

8. If one of your friends were suffering from this kind of depression, what advice would you give him or her? How effective do you think your advice would be? Explain.

9. How relevant do you think Psalm 4 is to people today? In other words, which emotions referred to by David in the psalm still affect people today? (Impatience [4:1], anger [4:2], confidence [4:3], trust [4:5], joy [4:7], contentment [4:8].)

10. **Most of David's psalms were written about situations in his personal life. Do you ever write to God about situations in your life? If so, what form does your writing take—journaling, poetry, humorous prose, or something else? Why? If not, why not? Is writing the only way to deal with your feelings? Explain.**

As a group, create a lullaby (perhaps to the tune of "Rockabye Baby") designed to help people sleep in peace, knowing that the Lord will keep them safe and provide for them. (For example, "Rock a bye, _____, in a bunk top/ When you can't sleep and you stare at the clock/When your head aches and you're feeling so small/ God will protect you and answer your call.") After singing the finished song a couple of times, close the session in prayer, thanking God for watching over us—both when we're awake and when we're asleep.

The Distractions

Sleepy Sam enters and sets up his bed to sleep. He is very tired, constantly yawning and stretching while he sleepily prepares for a good night's sleep. After setting up the bed, he lies down with a contented smile on his face.

Annoying Andrea, Sleepy Sam's oldest sister, enters as soon as Sleepy Sam falls asleep. She sits down next to Sam's bed, opens a bag of potato chips, and slowly crunches them between her teeth. She very noisily takes a swig of soda and bangs the can down on the floor.

Sleepy Sam sits up, startled, and then lies back down, pulling the covers over his head. *(Annoying Andrea leaves.)*

Irritating Ivan enters and sits down on Sam's bed. Ivan has a terrible cold. He blows his nose, coughs, and sneezes continually.

Sleepy Sam tosses and turns and finally kicks Ivan off the bed. *(Irritating Ivan leaves.)* Sam goes back to sleep.

Freda Flashlight, another of Sleepy Sam's sisters, enters, looking for something she lost. Using a flashlight, she searches all around and under Sam's bed, not realizing that Sam is in the bed. She accidentally shines the light in Sam's eyes. They both scream, and Freda runs out of the room.

Sleepy Sam disgustedly pulls the covers over his head again.

Noisy Nick enters, wearing a Walkman, and sits a few feet away from the bed. He keeps time with the music by beating two pencils together. He is so intent on his music that he doesn't notice Sam.

Sleepy Sam gets out of bed, grabs Nick by the back of his shirt, and throws him out. Then Sam climbs back into bed.

Chatty Cathy and Talky Tina, Sleepy Sam's two youngest sisters, enter, whispering quietly to each other, and sit next to Sam's bed. Their conversation grows more intense as they begin to talk louder and faster, until they both break into raucous laughter.

Sleepy Sam wearily gets up and drags his bed away.

PSALM 8

What a Wonderful World

OVERVIEW

David marvels at the majesty of God's creation and then expresses his amazement that God would grant humans the responsibility of caring for and ruling over His creation.

OPENING ACT

Have kids form six teams. Assign each team one of the days of creation described in Genesis 1. Instruct each team to come up with a screenplay for a five-minute video that shows what happened on its assigned day of creation. Instruct the teams to be as detailed as possible in their screenplays. Explain that you're looking for a shot-by-shot description of the video. Some teams may choose to use animation for their video; other teams (specifically the team assigned Day 6) may choose to use live actors in a dramatic recreation. Some teams may come up with a video that shows creation from God's point of view; others may come up with a video that shows creation from the point of view of something being created. After a few minutes, have each team share what it came up with. Then discuss as a group the approach of each screenplay. Afterward, point out that in this session, you're going to look at David's feelings concerning creation.

DATE I USED THIS SESSION _____ GROUP I USED IT WITH _____

NOTES FOR NEXT TIME _____

_____

_____

1. In your opinion, what's the coolest plant that God created? Why? What's the coolest animal that God created? Why? What's the coolest non-living thing that God created? Why?

2. Do you think most people today recognize the majesty and glory of God's creation? If not, why do you suppose that is?

3. Psalm 8:2 is quoted by Jesus in Matthew 21:16. What is it about this verse that's so significant? (Children seem to have a very special place in God's heart. Adults are encouraged to follow the example of children by praising God in a simple, innocent way that God delights in.)

4. What kinds of things do children praise God for (8:2) that adults and teenagers tend to overlook?

5. If you were to write a psalm about God's creation, what would you focus on? Why? What words—other than the ones used by David in Psalm 8—would you use to describe creation?

6. Have you ever received something you didn't deserve? If so, how did you feel about what you were given? How did you feel about the person who gave it to you? How might these feelings apply to David's questioning in Psalm 8:4?

7. How do you think God would answer David's question in Psalm 8:4—"What is man that you are mindful of him, the son of man that you care for him?"

8. How has God crowned humans "with glory and honor" (8:5)? What God-given qualities do we possess that distinguish us from other of God's creation? (Intelligence, emotion, free will, and creativity—among other things.)

9. As rulers over God's creation (8:6), what privileges do we enjoy? What responsibilities go along with being rulers over creation? Explain.

10. If we humans were to get a report card grading us on the job we've done in caring for God's earth, what grade do you think we would get? Explain. In what areas do we need to improve? In what areas are we doing a good job? Explain.

11. On a scale of one to ten—with ten being the highest—"how majestic is [God's] name in all the earth" (8:9) today? Explain.

Hand out copies of the reproducible sheet, "Home Maintenance." Give your group members a few minutes to find the hidden words and phrases. When everyone is finished, discuss as a group what, if any, responsibility Christians have to the environment. For instance, you might ask: **Why keep the earth clean if it's all going to be destroyed someday? Do some people make too big a deal out of environmental issues? Explain.** Afterward, discuss which of the ideas on the sheet your group members could begin working on. If possible, you might want to consider planning a group project to work on one or more of the ideas together. (For instance, you might organize a "Park Cleanup Day.")

Home Maintenance

Hidden in the word jumble below are several ideas on how to care for the "home" God has created for us. Your job is to find and circle them. (*Extra credit:* See how many characters from a popular TV show you can find.)

```
S  T  P  A  Y  G  R  E  N  E  E  V  R  E  S  N  O  C
T  U  P  A  C  L  E  A  N  P  A  R  K  S  U  Y  K  R
L  M  S  E  S  U  O  H  L  I  M  C  B  A  R  N  E  Y
P  E  F  E  L  C  Y  C  E  R  Y  O  K  D  R  M  N  A
P  N  B  L  B  P  S  M  I  T  H  E  R  S  O  A  R  N
C  O  E  S  E  I  R  A  O  T  C  S  V  H  N  A  E  C
U  S  H  I  L  C  O  Y  H  C  T  A  R  C  S  D  L  V
R  P  P  D  P  K  E  D  R  M  I  R  O  N  F  O  S  S
B  M  R  E  P  U  O  D  E  A  O  V  K  L  O  I  L  E
P  I  R  S  A  P  C  L  N  G  G  A  A  P  D  O  T  E
O  S  D  H  B  L  I  S  A  G  R  N  R  N  R  A  Y  R
L  N  H  O  A  I  R  F  I  I  D  A  M  A  R  G  E  T
L  R  E  W  R  T  O  E  K  E  C  Y  D  R  T  A  M  T
U  U  T  B  K  T  M  C  R  P  T  N  O  A  R  U  T  N
T  B  H  O  S  E  T  S  O  S  K  M  S  L  B  O  R  A
I  R  R  B  R  R  G  S  U  D  U  O  L  T  S  L  A  L
O  M  R  E  M  O  Y  R  E  F  R  E  T  R  A  B  E  P
N  R  E  N  N  I  K  S  L  A  P  I  C  N  I  R  P  S
```

Words to Find

Recycle	Pick up litter	Carpool	Curb pollution
Plant trees	Conserve energy	Clean parks	Use biodegradables

PSALM 10

Wicked Games

In Psalm 10, the psalmist prays for rescue from his oppressors. In describing his oppressors, the psalmist creates a very vivid portrait of wickedness. After struggling to understand why corrupt people believe that their evil deeds will go unnoticed by God, the psalmist affirms that God *will* judge the wicked. The psalmist then celebrates the fact that the Lord protects the afflicted and oppressed.

Hand out copies of the reproducible sheet, "Bad to the Bone." Give group members a few minutes to complete the sheet. When everyone is finished, ask volunteers to share and explain their rankings. Afterward, discuss briefly as a group what causes people to be wicked.

DATE I USED THIS SESSION _____ GROUP I USED IT WITH _____

NOTES FOR NEXT TIME _____

_____

_____

1. Who is the most wicked villain you've ever seen in a movie or TV show? What is it about the person that made him or her an effective villain? Explain.

2. Why do you think the psalmist feels far away from God in Psalm 10:1? (Perhaps because he sees the proliferation of evil around him, but doesn't see God doing anything about it.)

3. Do you know people who "[hunt] down the weak" (10:2)? Explain. If so, do you ever stand up to such people? Why or why not?

4. Does it ever seem to you that the ways of the wicked "are always prosperous" (10:5)? If so, why do you suppose that is?

5. Do you know anybody like the person described in Psalm 10:6? If so, what would you say to the person based on the information in the rest of the psalm?

6. Psalm 10:7 describes how wicked people use words for evil purposes. What are some ways in which we could use our words to help others and to build others up?

7. In what ways do wicked people "[lie] in wait to catch the helpless" (10:9)? What kind of people might be caught and dragged off by the wicked?

8. Do you ever feel as if God has "forgotten" (10:11) about the wicked, not punishing their evil deeds and even allowing them to prosper? Explain.

9. How does it make you feel to know that God *does* "see trouble and grief" and "[considers] it to take it in hand" (10:14)?

10. What do you think of the psalmist's request in Psalm 10:15 for God to "break the arm of the wicked and evil man"? If no one mentions it, point out that the psalmist is not advocating physical violence; instead, he is asking God to destroy the power of the wicked.

11. How would you simplify the psalmist's words in Psalm 10:16-18 if you were explaining the passage to a younger sibling or relative?

Briefly review Psalm 10:16-18. Suggest that your group members could get involved in helping the people described in the passage. Hand out paper and pencils. Ask group members to write down the names of two or three people they know who might be considered "afflicted" or "fatherless." Then have them write down at least five specific ways in which they could comfort, encourage, or help those people. After a few minutes, ask volunteers to share some of the suggestions they came up with. As you close the meeting, encourage your group members to put their ideas to work.

BAD to the Bone

Rank the following "villains" according to how evil you think they are—with the person you rank #1 being the most evil, the person you rank #2 being the second-most evil, and so on. (We've left one space blank for you to come up with your own villain.) Afterward, be prepared to explain and defend your rankings.

_____ An African tribal leader who won't allow donated food to be transported to starving people in another tribe

_____ A phony contractor who charges elderly people tremendous amounts of money to do work on their homes, but never does the work

_____ A drug dealer who sells marijuana, cocaine, heroin, and other narcotics to kids junior-high age and younger

_____ A terrorist who explodes a car bomb in a public square, killing five innocent bystanders

_____ A parent who emotionally and physically abuses his or her child

_____ A cult leader who convinces his followers that he is God and that they should dedicate their lives to him

_____ A classmate who convinces several people at school that someone has AIDS who really doesn't

_____ A pimp who hangs around bus stations and entices runaways to get involved in prostitution

_____ A televangelist who preys on elderly and gullible people, promising them God's blessings if they will send him their money

_____ A person filling out a sheet called "Bad to the Bone" who would rather be doing something else

_____ Other _____

PSALM 13

How Long?

OVERVIEW

Continuing to point out the godlessness all around him, David cries out to God. He begs for assurance from God, but feels abandoned by Him and defeated by the wickedness around him. David's misery and impatience seem too much for him to bear as he asks repeatedly, "How long?" in reference to his suffering. David's attitude changes when he remembers the goodness of the Lord, and he closes the psalm by singing victoriously to the Lord, thanking Him for salvation.

OPENING ACT

Hand out copies of the reproducible sheet, "Automatic Headlines." But before group members read the sheet, have each person write down a five-digit number. Then have group members go through the sheet to see what headline they created based on their five-digit number. After a few minutes, have each group member stand and read his or her headline aloud. (It's likely that some of the headlines will be pretty humorous.) Afterward, have group members read Psalm 13; then have them go back through the sheet and come up with an actual headline for the Bible passage. (Possible headlines might include "Impatient David Accuses the Wicked in the World" [47,761] and "Humble King Praises Creator during Prayer" [14,085].)

DATE I USED THIS SESSION _____ GROUP I USED IT WITH _____

NOTES FOR NEXT TIME _____

_____

_____

1. Have you ever felt forgotten or abandoned by your parents or friends? If so, what were the circumstances? How did you feel about the person or persons who forgot or abandoned you? How did you resolve the situation?

2. What kinds of things might cause a person to feel as if God has forgotten about him or her (13:1)? How do you suppose that feels?

3. What kinds of thoughts do kids your age "wrestle" with? How would you respond to someone who asked you, "How long must I wrestle with my thoughts?" (13:2)?

4. David seemed to struggle a lot with the problem of his enemies triumphing over him (13:2). Do you think Christ's command to "Love your enemies" (Matthew 5:44) makes Christians more vulnerable or less vulnerable to attack from their enemies? Explain.

5. David repeats the question, "How long?" four times in Psalm 13:1, 2. Why do you think he was so impatient for the Lord to work? Have you ever been impatient for the Lord to work in your life? If so, what were the circumstances? How did the situation turn out?

6. Why do you think the Lord allowed David to be besieged by his enemies? If David was a man after God's own heart, why didn't God just give him the power to defeat his enemies anytime they oppressed him? (Perhaps God was teaching David patience. Perhaps he was showing David the need to depend on Him.)

7. Why do you think David was so concerned that his enemies not be able to say they had overcome him (13:4)? Do you think it was a matter of pride? Explain. (Perhaps David was afraid that in defeating him, God's chosen king, his enemies would try to claim victory over God.)

8. In the first four verses of Psalm 13, David doesn't seem very trusting. But in verse 5, he says to God, "I trust in your unfailing love." How do you explain David's abrupt change of attitude?

9. Without saying, "Love that never fails," how would you define or describe "unfailing love"?

10. David promises to sing to celebrate the Lord's goodness to him (13:6). What do you do to celebrate the Lord's goodness to you? Explain.

11. What kinds of things keep some people from celebrating the Lord's goodness? Explain.

Hand out paper and pencils. Have group members write down at least three things that they've been wrestling with for quite some time. These things might include sorrows, unanswered questions, personal problems, and other issues. Then have group members write down approximately how long they've been struggling with each area. When everyone is finished, have group members pair up (preferably with someone they know pretty well). Have each person share with his or her partner what would need to happen in order for each situation on his or her list to be resolved. As you wrap up the session, have the members of each pair pray together for each other's situations. If you think your group members would be uncomfortable sharing with each other, simply have them pray silently about the areas they identify.

Automatic *Headlines*

You're a reporter for *The Daily Scroll*, a local newspaper in Jerusalem. You've been assigned to cover the events in Psalm 13 and now you're trying to create a headline for your story. The problem is that since the newspaper's computers have been updated, all key words for headlines have been converted to a number code. But you don't know the code, so you simply type in five numbers and hope for the best. Based on the five-digit number you wrote down earlier, what headline did you come up with? (In the first box, circle the first number of your five-digit number; in the second box, circle the second number; etc. Then read the words that are circled to come up with your headline.)

BOX 1
0—FORGETFUL
1—HUMBLE
2—SINFUL
3—WARM-HEARTED
4—IMPATIENT
5—HUNGRY
6—RIGHTEOUS
7—DOUBLE-JOINTED
8—LUCKY
9—DESPERATE

BOX 2
0—TAX COLLECTOR
1—EMBALMER
2—FISHERMAN
3—CHOIR MEMBER
4—KING
5—RABBI
6—MUSICIAN
7—DAVID
8—BRICKLAYER
9—STONECUTTER

BOX 3
0—PRAISES
1—CROWNS
2—KISSES
3—INSULTS
4—BETRAYS
5—EXECUTES
6—TRAMPLES
7—ACCUSES
8—FORGIVES
9—HEALS

BOX 4
0—TRUMPETERS
1—PRIESTS
2—LEPERS
3—BABIES
4—CRIMINALS
5—ROMAN SOLDIERS
6—THE WICKED
7—GOATS
8—CREATOR
9—CHOIR

BOX 5
0—ON ROOF OF HOUSE
1—IN THE WORLD
2—IN THE GARDEN
3—IN THE DESERT
4—AT JEWISH FEAST
5—DURING PRAYER
6—IN THE WELL
7—IN THE BURIAL TOMB
8—IN THE KING'S PALACE
9—IN THE TEMPLE CHARIOT

PSALM 14

What a Fool Believes

In Psalm 14, David again describes the actions and attitudes of fools and evildoers. He then asserts that God is present among righteous people. At the end of the psalm, David longs for the day when Israel will be completely delivered from its enemies.

Hand out copies of the reproducible sheet, "Fools 'R' Us." Give group members a few minutes to complete the sheet. When everyone is finished, ask volunteers to share their responses. Use this activity to lead in to a discussion on the "foolish" people described by David in Psalm 14.

DATE I USED THIS SESSION _____ GROUP I USED IT WITH _____

NOTES FOR NEXT TIME _____

_____

_____

1. What's the most foolish thing you've ever done? What made it so foolish? What, if anything, did you learn from it?

2. When people use the word *fool* today, what are they referring to? (*Webster's New Collegiate Dictionary* defines *fool* as "a person lacking in judgment or prudence.") **How is that usage similar to or different from the use of the word in Psalm 14:1?**

3. Why is it foolish for a person to say, "There is no God" (14:1)? (Among other things, it requires ignoring or denying the evidence of God found throughout nature.)

4. According to Psalm 14:1, would you say it's impossible for an atheist to do good deeds? Explain.

5. How do you think the Lord feels about what He sees when He "looks down from heaven" (14:2, 3)? Explain.

6. What kind of understanding do you think God is looking for in Psalm 14:2? What does it mean to "seek" Him?

7. What do you think it would take to make "evildoers" learn the error of their wicked ways (14:4)? Why doesn't God just teach them once and for all the lessons they need to learn?

8. What are some ways in which evildoers might "devour" God's people (14:4)? Describe a time when you felt "chewed up" and persecuted by non-Christians. What were the circumstances? How did you feel? What happened?

9. What people might be especially comforted by the promise in Psalm 14:5 that "God is present in the company of the righteous"? Anyone who answers, "the righteous," has to stay after the meeting to clean up the room all by himself or herself.

10. Why do you think God allows evildoers to "frustrate the plans of the poor" (14:6)? (In a sense, He's giving the "poor" an opportunity to turn to Him to rest in the safety of His refuge and to witness His power on their behalf.)

11. Describe a time in your life when you experienced God as a refuge from evildoers. What were the circumstances? How was the situation resolved? How did the experience affect your relationship with God?

Refer group members back to Psalm 14:2—"The Lord looks down from heaven on the sons [and daughters] of men to see if there are any who . . . seek God." Ask: **When the Lord looks down on you, does He see someone who seeks Him and His will in all areas of life?** Give group members a moment to silently consider the question. If group members are honest with themselves, they'll probably admit that there are at least a few areas of their lives in which they don't necessarily seek God's will. Hand out paper and pencils. Have group members write down at least two or three areas in their lives in which they don't usually seek God's will, as well as the reasons for not seeking God's will in those areas. Then have group members write down what might need to happen for them to be able to turn those areas over to God. As you wrap up the session, emphasize that God wants—and knows—what's best for us in *all* areas of our life.

FOOLS 'R' US

In the thought balloons below, write down what you think each character might say about God, based on his or her description. Use some creativity and humor in your answers. (After all, you wouldn't want someone to think you're a fool, would you?)

HARLEY
Harley likes to ride fast and start fights. In his opinion, Christianity is for wimps and nuns.

PRISCILLA
Priscilla enjoys her popularity and is too busy with "important" people to waste her time hanging around unpopular Christian kids.

LARRY
Larry letters in three sports. He lifts weights for two hours a day to stay fit and toned. He doesn't have time for God. Besides, he doesn't trust anything he can't do on his own.

SKYY
Skyy is into the earth and environmental issues. She sees no need for organized religion when she can "be one" with nature.

JUANITA
Juanita knows more than most of her teachers—and often points out that fact. Her intelligence doesn't allow her to, in her words, "entertain the superstitious"— including God.

ARMSTRONG
Armstrong was born into country- club society. He's rich, arrogant, snobby, and elitist. To him, Christianity is for "lower class" people who don't have culture.

PSALM 18

Solid Rock

OVERVIEW

It seems that David's previous psalmic prayers and pleas to God for protection from his enemies have paid off. In Psalm 18, David gives praise to the Lord—His rock, fortress, and deliverer—after being delivered from foreign enemies as well as from Saul. David describes not only the wrath of the Lord upon his enemies, but also his deliverance from those enemies. David closes the psalm with a description of the various blessings he has received from God.

OPENING ACT

(Needed: Hand lotion, stopwatch)

Have group members form pairs. One at a time, have each pair come to the front of the room. Explain that you're going to have a contest to see which set of partners can hold on to each other's hands for the longest amount of time. The catch is that before grabbing hands, the members of each pair must coat their hands with hand lotion. Ask two of your strongest group members to serve as "pullers." After the members of each pair apply the lotion and grab hands, the pullers will try to pull them apart. Using a stopwatch, time how long it takes for each pair to be separated. The pair that stays together the longest is the winner. Afterward, point out that David had someone in his life that he could *always* cling to.

DATE I USED THIS SESSION _____ GROUP I USED IT WITH _____

NOTES FOR NEXT TIME _____

_____

_____

1. Describe the toughest situation or problem you've ever gotten out of. What were the circumstances? How did you get out of it?

2. David praises God as his strength (18:1), his rock, his fortress, his deliverer, his refuge, his shield, and his stronghold (18:2). What do these descriptions tell you about David's situation at the time he wrote this psalm? (Many of the descriptions are military in nature—which is appropriate, since the Lord had delivered David from his military enemies.)

3. If you were to praise God for His work in your life recently, what kinds of descriptions would you use? Explain.

4. David affirms that God is "worthy of praise" (18:3). Why do you think some people neglect to praise God for the things He's done in their lives? What could you do to establish a habit of praising God for His work in your life?

5. The description of God's actions on behalf of David is pretty dramatic (18:7-19). If you'd been one of David's enemies, how do you think you would have responded after seeing God's work?

6. Do you think God still works in such spectacular, awe-inspiring ways today? Explain. Do you think natural disasters like earthquakes and floods might be the result of God's anger against today's sinful society? Explain.

7. What "foes" in your life are "too strong" for you (18:17)? How might God rescue you from such foes?

8. In Psalm 18:19, David says, "[The Lord] rescued me because he delighted in me." Think about your life right now. Would you say that the Lord "delights" in you? Why or why not? If not, what might you do to cause the Lord to delight in you?

9. According to Psalm 18:25, 26, the Lord shows Himself faithful to the faithful—but to the crooked, He shows Himself shrewd. What do you think that means? (Those who are faithful to God will discover that He is faithful to them; those who don't follow the Lord will discover that He is just.)

10. In what areas of life are people your age tempted to be "haughty" or cocky and arrogant? Why? How might God "bring low" those people (18:27)? Explain.

11. David closes the psalm by describing the various blessings that God has bestowed on him (18:32-50). If you were to list the various blessings that God has bestowed on you, what kinds of things would your list include? Explain.

Hand out copies of the reproducible sheet, "What a Rock!" Let group members work in pairs or small groups to complete the sheet. When everyone is finished, go through the answers as a group. (Suggested answers are as follows: [1] Serves as a shield and the horn of salvation; [2] Shakes mountains when angry; [3] Breathes fire and smoke; [4] Flies; [5] Shoots arrows and bolts of lightning; [6] Rescues and supports; [7] Turns darkness into light; [8] Trains people for battle; [9] Prevents injuries; [10] Subdues nations and saves people from their enemies.) Afterward, ask: **Which of God's attributes described by David in Psalm 18 is most impressive to you? Explain. Which means the most to you right now? Why?** Close the session in prayer, thanking God that He is always available for us to "cling to."

WHAT A ROCK!

Several years ago—during the weird and wonderful 1970s—"pet rocks" were the most popular novelty items available. It seemed like everyone owned a pet rock. Many owners claimed that their rocks had special abilities and talents. (People were easily amused in the 1970s.) But no pet rock could even come close to matching the rock described by David in Psalm 18. Read through the verses listed below to come up with a list of the characteristics and attributes of David's "Rock." The first one has been completed for you.

TOP TEN CHARACTERISTICS/ATTRIBUTES OF DAVID'S ROCK

1. *Psalm 18:2*—Serves as a shield and the horn of salvation

2. *Psalm 18:7*—

3. *Psalm 18:8*—

4. *Psalm 18:10*—

5. *Psalm 18:14*—

6. *Psalm 18:17, 18*—

7. *Psalm 18:28*—

8. *Psalm 18:34*—

9. *Psalm 18:36*—

10. *Psalm 18:47, 48*—

PSALM 19

Star Search

OVERVIEW

After praising God for delivering him from the hands of his enemies, David reflects on God's glory, displayed through His creation of the heavens as well as through His Word, which details the laws and principles the Lord wants His people to live by. David closes the psalm by asking God for forgiveness for his sins and pleading that his thoughts and actions will be acceptable to God.

OPENING ACT

(Needed: Several unusual objects)

Display several objects that have something unusual about them. For instance, you might bring in a shoe that's been chewed by a dog, a book with its cover torn off, a container that was melted in a microwave, or a piece that was broken off a toy. Have kids form pairs. Instruct each pair to choose three objects to "explain." The pairs should offer an explanation as to what can be deduced about each object based on its appearance and then offer a theory as to how the object came to be in the condition it's in. Encourage kids to be as creative and humorous as possible in their explanations and theories. After a few minutes, have each pair share what it came up with. Afterward, explain that in this session, you'll discover what David deduced about God based on God's handiwork.

DATE I USED THIS SESSION _____ GROUP I USED IT WITH _____

NOTES FOR NEXT TIME _____

_____

_____

1. Finish this sentence: "You can tell a lot about a person based on his or her _____." What can these things tell us about a person? Explain.

2. Finish this sentence: "You can tell a lot about God based on _____." What can these things tell us about God? Explain.

3. How do "the heavens declare the glory of God" and "the skies proclaim the work of his hands" (19:1)? (Things like clouds and the sky are so incredibly and beautifully designed that they point to God, their Creator, and His handi-work.)

4. Why do you think some people are unable or unwilling to recognize the work of God in His creation? (Perhaps they are too busy to even notice God's creation. Perhaps they are so used to seeing things like clouds and the sky that they're not impressed anymore.)

5. Compare Psalm 19:3, 4 with Romans 1:20. Based on these two passages, why are things like clouds and the sky so important? (For some people, these and other aspects of creation are an introduction to God Himself. In areas of the world where there are no Bibles, nature serves as a testimony to the existence of a Creator.)

6. After talking about the majesty of God's creation, David considers the power and beauty of God's Word (Psalm 19:7-11). Why do you suppose God's creation and His Word are so closely related in this psalm? (They both reveal aspects of God.)

7. What kinds of things are capable of "giving joy to [your] heart" (19:8)? Would you include God's Word among those things? Why or why not?

8. How might someone who believes that God's Word is more precious than gold (19:10) live his or her life to demonstrate that belief? (The person might build his or her schedule around his or her Bible study time. The person might also try to "share the wealth" of God's Word with others.)

9. **Why do you think David prayed for forgiveness for his "hidden faults"** (19:12)**?** (Sometimes people commit sins without realizing what they've done. David didn't want such sins to interfere with his relationship with God.)

10. **What's the difference between a "willful"** (19:13) **sin and other kinds of sin?** (A willful sin might be considered a premeditated or habitual sin—in other words, open rebellion against God.)

11. **If you were to genuinely pray David's words in Psalm 19:14, how do you think your life might change? Explain.**

Hand out copies of the reproducible sheet, "Get a Clue." Give group members a few minutes to complete the sheet. When everyone is finished, ask volunteers to share their responses. Then ask group members to name their five favorite creations of God and explain why those creations are their favorites. Close the session in prayer, thanking God for giving us clues—in nature and in His Word—as to what He's like, and asking Him to help us pay attention to such clues so that we may learn more about Him.

Get a Clue

We can get clues as to what God is like simply by looking around at the things He's created. For each of the following creations of God, write down some things we might be able to tell about God based on that creation.

Volcano	Dinosaur	Mosquito

Shark	**Solar system**	**Aardvark**

Skunk	**Human beings**	**Flowers**

PSALM 22

No Pain, No Gain

In the midst of being persecuted by unprovoked enemies, David cries out to God. He pours out his feelings of abandonment and despair, and describes in figurative language the suffering he's experienced. Then as David reflects on God's previous deliverances of His people, he begins hoping again. This fragile hope rekindles David's confidence and helps him understand that suffering has a point—a fact he vows to proclaim to his people.

(Needed: Costumes [optional])

Ask for two volunteers to act out a brief skit. Give each volunteer a copy of the reproducible sheet, "Pump U Up." If possible, try to have some costumes available for your actors. (You could use oversized sweatsuits stuffed with towels.) Give the actors a minute or two to look over the script; then have them perform. When they're finished, give them a round of applause. Then ask: **When it comes to working out, do you believe the expression "No pain, no gain" is true? Why or why not? Do you think the expression is true of the Christian life? Why or why not?**

DATE I USED THIS SESSION _____ GROUP I USED IT WITH _____

NOTES FOR NEXT TIME _____

_____

_____

1. What is the most intense physical pain you've ever experienced? What were the circumstances? How did you deal with the pain? How long did it take for the pain to go away?

2. Which is easier to deal with—physical pain or emotional pain? Explain.

3. Describe a time in your life when you were tempted to echo David's question in Psalm 22:1: "My God, my God, why have you forsaken me?" Why do you think people feel abandoned by God when they encounter tough times?

4. Read Matthew 27:46. **Why do you think Jesus used these words as He was being crucified?** (When Jesus took upon Himself the sins of mankind, God, in His holiness, turned away from His Son. This separation was so devastating to Jesus that He quoted David's words in Psalm 22:1.)

5. If you were feeling abandoned and ignored by God, do you think it would help you to recall things the Lord had done for other people (22:4, 5)? Why or why not? Do you think it helped David? Explain.

6. David uses several animal illustrations in this psalm (22:6, 12, 13, 16). **What do you think each one symbolizes?** (The worm probably represents the lowliness that David feels. The bulls might represent the strength of the people who oppose David. The lions might represent the viciousness of David's opponents. The dogs might represent the tenacity of David's enemies.)

7. After David describes his pitiful position in life, he asks God for deliverance (22:19-21). **What seems to be David's attitude after asking for God's help?** (He seems to be relatively sure that God will help him because he starts making plans to praise and worship God [22:22].)

8. Why do you think David was so sure that God would deliver him? (Perhaps because of God's "track record" for delivering David in the past.)

9. What causes people today to doubt that God will deliver them from difficult situations in their life?

10. When was the last time you shared with other people—as David describes in Psalm 22:22—something God had done for you? Why are some people hesitant to share with others the things that God has done for them?

(Needed: Chalkboard and chalk or newsprint and marker)

As a group, brainstorm a list of situations that might cause a person to feel alienated from God. Try to come up with as many situations as possible. Write the situations on the board as group members call them out. Then brainstorm a list of ways in which God might deliver a person from—or help a person deal with—such situations. Emphasize that God may not choose to eliminate a particular situation from a person's life, but He will give that person strength and wisdom to deal with the situation. Close the session in prayer, thanking God that He remains close to us even when we don't sense His closeness.

Pump U Up

HANS: My name is Hans. *(He flexes.)*

FRANZ: And my name is Franz. *(He flexes.)*

BOTH: And we're here to pump *(clap)* you up.

HANS: This is our personal training session for people who are tired of being girly-men.

FRANZ: Yah. Maybe if you train every day for the rest of your pathetic life you will achieve one-tenth of the pumptitude that we have.

(Both flex.)

HANS: Remember our slogan: "No pain, no gain." Franz will demonstrate our first exercise—the stomach crunch.

(Franz does one situp and then holds the pose, all the while flexing and grimacing wildly.)

HANS: All you girly-men at home should feel the burn of this exercise after only two seconds. Do you feel the burn, Franz?

FRANZ: Yah. We could fry three eggs and a side order of bacon using the burn I feel from this exercise.

HANS: Franz and I often must change clothes during a workout because we burn our muscles so intensely that our shirts catch on fire.

FRANZ *(Standing up):* That is a hazard you girly-men need not worry about. Your burn could not melt an ice cube. Hans will now demonstrate our second exercise—bicep curls.

(Hans begins flexing his biceps and grimacing wildly.)

FRANZ: If you do not feel pain during this exercise, you are not doing it right. Your little girly-man muscles must be destroyed and replaced with new ones.

HANS *(Continuing to flex):* Although you can never hope to attain the massiveness that we have.

FRANZ: Do you feel the pain yet, Hans?

HANS: Yah. Most men would die from the pain I'm experiencing now.

FRANZ: We are almost out of time, so remember, you girly-men—no pain, no gain.

HANS: Yah. We will see you on our next show.

FRANZ: And if you do not watch our next show, we will hunt you down and pull your flabby little stomach muscles over your head so that you must look through your belly button to see.

HANS: Yah. And remember, my name is Hans. *(He flexes.)*

FRANZ: And my name is Franz. *(He flexes.)*

BOTH: And we're here to pump *(clap)* you up.

PSALM 23

Have Shepherd, Will Travel

OVERVIEW

While David has struggled with feeling distant from God in the midst of adversity, he seems to understand that those "suffering" times are meant to help him lean on God even more in his life. David professes that he will trust in God, likening God to a shepherd who brings peace, comfort, and security to his sheep.

OPENING ACT

(Needed: Masking tape, golf balls, wastebasket, stopwatch)

Begin the session with "The Shepherd Game." Tape a large square on the floor. Place a wastebasket in the middle of the square. Choose one "shepherd" at a time to participate. Have the contestant stand next to the wastebasket (the "sheep pen"). Then spread out several (30-40) golf balls on the floor inside the square. Explain that the golf balls represent stray sheep. The shepherd's job is to put all of the "stray sheep" into the "pen" as quickly as possible. The shepherd who gets all of the golf balls into the wastebasket in the shortest amount of time is the winner. Use this activity to lead in to a discussion of David's shepherd in Psalm 23.

DATE I USED THIS SESSION _____ GROUP I USED IT WITH _____

NOTES FOR NEXT TIME _____

_____

_____

1. What do you want more than anything else in the world? Why? How would you feel if you never got it? Explain.

2. What do you think David means when he says, "The Lord is my shepherd, I shall not be in want" (23:1)? (David is saying that the Lord will provide for him and take care of his needs. With the Lord as his shepherd, David will be able to enjoy "goodness" in his life [23:6].)

3. Based on Psalm 23:1, do you think it's wrong for a Christian to desire things? Explain.

4. Why do you think David chose to describe God as a "shepherd" (23:1)? (David himself was a shepherd, so it was an occupation he knew well.) **In what ways is God a shepherd to His people?** (He leads us in the paths we should go; He protects us from "invaders"; He provides for our needs; etc.)

5. If you were to compare God to a person in a certain occupation, what occupation would you choose? Explain.

6. David was able to relax "in green pastures" and "beside quiet waters" (23:2). When you need to get away from everything and "recharge your batteries," where do you go? Why? Why is it important to periodically "get away from it all"? (In today's hurried and stressful society, we need time to quiet our hearts and reflect upon God.)

7. How do you think the "paths of righteousness" (vs. 3) differ from the paths of unrighteousness? (The paths of righteousness may be more difficult to travel, but their destination is much more desirable than the destination of the paths of unrighteousness.)

8. What is significant about the phrase "for His name's sake" in Psalm 23:3? (God guides us into right choices because He wants to be glorified through our actions. If we are His "sheep," then we represent Him, the "Great Shepherd," to the whole world.)

9. How do you think most people approach tough times in their life? Explain. How did David approach the time he would spend in the "valley of the shadow of death" (23:4)? (He was ready to confront such situations bravely, knowing that God was with him.)

10. A rod was an instrument used by a shepherd to direct and control his sheep. Why do you think such a device would be of "comfort" to David (23:4)? (It appears that David recognized the importance of the Lord's discipline in his life.)

11. What blessings from God might cause your "cup" to overflow (23:5)?

Give your group members an opportunity to "customize" Psalm 23 to fit their own life situations. Hand out copies of the reproducible sheet, "My Psalm 23." Give group members a few minutes to complete the sheet. When everyone is finished, ask volunteers to share parts of their customized psalms with the rest of the group. Close the session in prayer, thanking God for "shepherding" us through the difficult times in our lives.

My Psalm 23

Psalm 23 is a powerful Scripture passage, but it's written from David's point of view—with his circumstances and feelings in mind. Here's your chance to "customize" the psalm to fit your circumstances and feelings. Simply complete the statements below.

The Lord is my shepherd, which means a lot to me because . . .

I shall not be in want of things like . . .

He makes me lie down in green pastures and leads me beside quiet waters, giving me a quiet place to rest and "recharge" when . . .

He restores my soul by . . .

He guides me in the paths of righteousness, helping me make God-honoring decisions about things like . . .

Even though I walk through the valley of the shadow of death or face other scary situations like . . .

I will fear no evil, for You are with me. I know this for sure because . . .

Your rod and your staff, they comfort me—even when they discipline me for doing things like . . .

You prepare a table for me in the presence of my enemies. If it weren't for You, my enemies would probably . . .

You anoint my head with oil; my cup overflows with blessings like . . .

Surely goodness and love will follow me all the days of my life, and I will dwell in the house of the Lord forever. I look forward to this because . . .

PSALM 25

Talkin' 'bout God

David prays with a sense of awe and fearful reverence to the all-powerful God, reminding the Lord of His mercy, love, goodness, uprightness, faithfulness, and grace—and appealing to those qualities to save him (David) from his enemies.

Begin the session with "The Compliment Game." Have group members sit in a circle. Introduce an imaginary person—Mr. Bigg—to the group. Explain that Mr. Bigg is an employer with a great-paying job for a teenager. The key to getting the job, however, is to "butter up" Mr. Bigg, complimenting him in a creative and unusual way. Choose a group member to go first. Give him or her five seconds to compliment some area of Mr. Bigg's life, using the letter "A" (for example, "I'll bet you're an *awesome artist*"). The next person then has five seconds to come up with a compliment using the letter "B" ("I'll bet you're a *brilliant barber*"). Continue in this manner around the circle, using successive letters of the alphabet. If someone cannot think of a compliment in five seconds, he or she is out. The last person remaining is the winner. Afterward, explain that in this session, you're going to be looking at a psalm in which some might say David appears to be trying to "butter up" God—appealing to the Lord's mercy, love, and grace to rescue David from his enemies.

DATE I USED THIS SESSION _____ GROUP I USED IT WITH _____

NOTES FOR NEXT TIME _____

_____

_____

1. What's the greatest compliment you've ever received in your life? Who gave you the compliment? How did you respond? Did the compliment change your attitude toward the person who complimented you? If so, how?

2. What's the deal with David and his enemies? Every time you turn around in the Book of Psalms, it seems like David is asking God for deliverance from his enemies (25:2). Why doesn't God just get rid of David's enemies once and for all? (Perhaps God is teaching David to remain dependent on Him for David's needs.)

3. Have you ever seen a "treacherous" or troublemaking person "put to shame" (25:3)? If so, what were the circumstances? How did it make you feel? Why?

4. What might keep some people from praying David's words in Psalm 25:4, 5—"Show me your ways, O Lord, teach me your paths; guide me in your truth"? In other words, why might some people not want to be taught or guided by the Lord?

5. Do you think it's fair for David to ask the Lord to "Remember [His] great mercy and love," but to "Remember not the sins of [David's] youth" (25:6, 7)? Why or why not?

6. Read Psalm 25:8-15. Does it seem to you like David is trying to "butter up" the Lord in this passage—perhaps so that the Lord will answer David's request? Explain.

7. If you were to give God the greatest compliment you can think of, what would it be? Explain.

8. Do you think the Lord is more likely to honor a person's prayer request if the person first praises God before making the request? Explain.

9. What do you think David means by "The Lord confides in those who fear him" (25:14)? (The Lord treats people who obey Him as friends.) What do you think it would mean for you personally to be taken into the Lord's confidence? Explain.

10. **How might David's prayer in Psalm 25 be an encouragement to us when we face difficult times?** (It might reassure us that the all-powerful, all-loving God is ready, willing, and able to help us with any and all of our problems—no matter how oppressive those problems may seem.)

Hand out copies of the reproducible sheet, "A to Z." Let group members work in small groups to complete the sheet. After a few minutes, have each group read what it came up with. Then have each person choose one quality or mercy of God that is especially meaningful to him or her right now and praise God for it during a time of prayer with his or her group.

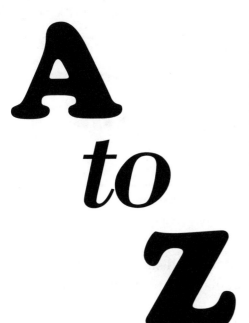

In appealing to God in Psalm 25 to save him from his enemies, David lists several qualities and mercies of the Lord ("Good and upright is the Lord" [25:8], "He guides the humble in what is right" [25:9]). If you were to appeal to God to help you in some way, which of His qualities and mercies would you list? See if you can come up with 26 qualities and mercies of God, using every letter of the alphabet. [NOTE: Each letter may appear *anywhere* in a word—not necessarily at the beginning.]

_____ A _____
_____ B _____
_____ C _____
_____ D _____
_____ E _____
_____ F _____
_____ G _____
_____ H _____
_____ I _____
_____ J _____
_____ K _____
_____ L _____
_____ M _____
_____ N _____
_____ O _____
_____ P _____
_____ Q _____
_____ R _____
_____ S _____
_____ T _____
_____ U _____
_____ V _____
_____ W _____
_____ X _____
_____ Y _____
_____ Z _____

PSALM 27

The Waiting Game

In earlier psalms, David prayed fearfully and reverently for the mercy of the all-loving, all-powerful God. In Psalm 27, David seems to grow in confidence, "seeing the light" of having God in control of his life. David states that no matter what the circumstances are, we have no reason to fear because the Lord is on our side.

(Needed: Wastebasket, paper wads)

Begin the session with a game of "Fear," which is played like the basketball game "Horse." Set up a wastebasket in the middle of the room. Give each group member a paper wad. Assign the order in which group members will shoot. If a person makes a basket on his or her shot, the next person must make the same shot from the same location. If the second person misses, he or she is given a letter (F, E, A, R). When a person gets four letters, he or she is out of the game. The last person remaining (or the person with the fewest letters when time is called) is the winner. Afterward, lead in to a discussion of what David says about fear in Psalm 27.

DATE I USED THIS SESSION _____ GROUP I USED IT WITH _____

NOTES FOR NEXT TIME _____

_____

_____

1. What's the scariest thing that's ever happened to you? How did you respond? How do you usually react when you're scared or nervous about something? Why?

2. David said the Lord was his "light and . . . salvation" (27:1). What words would you use to describe the Lord?

3. Why do you think David was so confident that the Lord would protect him from the advances of "evil men" (27:2)? (The Lord had protected David several times before in the midst of difficult situations.)

4. Complete the following sentence: "One thing I ask of the Lord, this is what I seek . . ." Compare group members' responses with David's words in Psalm 27:4.

5. What do you think David is talking about in Psalm 27:4? (David is requesting protection and fellowship with the Lord for the rest of his life. He is also requesting the wisdom and desire to seek God when difficult times arise.)

6. Obviously, David had a few "frightening" experiences in his lifetime that he could look back on. How many of them can you think of? (Among other things, David battled a lion, a bear, and the giant Goliath. He also faced several attempts on his life by King Saul.)

7. Why is it important that when God comes to our aid, we thank Him with shouts of joy, singing, and music (27:6)? (The Lord desires for us to praise Him, which shows our love for Him.)

8. Do you see any significance in the fact that David asks the Lord to be "merciful" to him (27:7)? Explain. (Mercy is compassion that is shown to a person who doesn't deserve it. David doesn't pretend to assume that he *deserves* protection from the Lord; he recognizes that the Lord will protect him only because the Lord is merciful and full of grace.)

9. In Psalm 27:10, what does the phrase, "Though my father and mother forsake me, the Lord will receive me," mean to you? (Our hope should be put in God, because if we put it in humans—even if those humans are our parents—those people will fail us, because human nature is sinful.)

10. How would you explain Psalm 27:14 to a friend who is facing some seriously difficult situations in his or her life?

Hand out copies of the reproducible sheet, "Fear-O-Meter." Give group members a few minutes to rate the various situations according to how much fear the situations might provoke in their lives. Then have group members write down an actual fear-provoking situation that they're currently facing. When everyone is finished, have group members pair up. Ask the members of each pair to read Psalm 27:14 and discuss what it might mean to "wait for the Lord" in the fear-provoking situations they're currently facing. Afterward, close the session in prayer, asking God for the wisdom and patience to "wait" for Him.

Fear-O-Meter

Shade in the "fear-o-meters" below to indicate how scary the following situations would be (or have been) to you. Then write down an actual fear-provoking situation that you're currently facing and shade in the fear-o-meter for it.

1. One of your parents takes a job in a different state, and your family has to move right away.

| 1 | 2 | 3 | 4 | 5 | 6 | 7 | 8 | 9 | 10 |

2. Your best friend says he or she is tired of hanging around with you and wants to spend time with more popular people.

| 1 | 2 | 3 | 4 | 5 | 6 | 7 | 8 | 9 | 10 |

3. A local gang starts trying to recruit you to join. The last person who refused was severely beaten.

| 1 | 2 | 3 | 4 | 5 | 6 | 7 | 8 | 9 | 10 |

4. Everyone ignores you on your first day at a new school.

| 1 | 2 | 3 | 4 | 5 | 6 | 7 | 8 | 9 | 10 |

5. You're asked to give a fifteen-minute speech at an assembly for your entire school.

| 1 | 2 | 3 | 4 | 5 | 6 | 7 | 8 | 9 | 10 |

6. Your grandmother is diagnosed as having terminal cancer. The doctors say she only has a few months to live.

| 1 | 2 | 3 | 4 | 5 | 6 | 7 | 8 | 9 | 10 |

7. Your parents announce that they're getting a divorce.

| 1 | 2 | 3 | 4 | 5 | 6 | 7 | 8 | 9 | 10 |

8. Your boyfriend or girlfriend tells you that he or she "just wants to be friends."

| 1 | 2 | 3 | 4 | 5 | 6 | 7 | 8 | 9 | 10 |

9. You've been diagnosed with a terminal illness. You have one year to live.

| 1 | 2 | 3 | 4 | 5 | 6 | 7 | 8 | 9 | 10 |

10. _____

| 1 | 2 | 3 | 4 | 5 | 6 | 7 | 8 | 9 | 10 |

PSALM 29

What a Voice!

In earlier psalms, David affirmed that with God on our side, we have nothing to fear. In Psalm 29, David attempts to put God's power into words so that others may understand the strength and might of the Almighty God.

Hand out copies of the reproducible sheet, "What a Disaster!" Give group members a few minutes to complete the sheet. When everyone is finished, go through the answers as a group. (The correct answers are as follows: [1] a; [2] d; [3] b; [4] e; [5] c; [6] c; [7] d; [8] b; [9] b; [10] a; [11] b; [12] a; [13] b; [14] c; [15] e.) Award prizes to group members who come up with all of the correct answers. Afterward, ask group members to talk about any experiences they or someone they know has had with natural disasters. Then point out that David compared the voice of the Lord to several such disasters to demonstrate just how powerful the Lord really is.

DATE I USED THIS SESSION _____ GROUP I USED IT WITH _____

NOTES FOR NEXT TIME _____

_____

_____

1. Who's the most famous person you've ever met in your life? How did you act when you met the person? Why? If you were able to meet the President of the United States or some other world leader, how do you think you would treat that person? Would you be in awe? Why or why not?

2. Do you think most people are "in awe" of God today? Why or why not? (Some people may tend to take God for granted, simply asking Him to do things for them—treating Him like a servant.)

3. What does it mean to "ascribe" something (29:1)? What should we ascribe to the Lord? ("Ascribe" means to attribute something to its source. We should ascribe to the Lord glory and strength.)

4. What is glory? (Praise or honor.) What glory is due God's name (29:2)? In other words, for what kinds of things does God deserve glory?

5. David talks about the voice of the Lord breaking the cedars of Lebanon and stripping the forests bare (29:5, 9). If you were trying to communicate the same message today, what examples might you use? Explain. (Smashing Mount Rushmore into pieces; uprooting all of the trees in Yellowstone National Park.)

6. The voice of the Lord is also compared to things such as lightning, shaking deserts, and floods. Why do you think David uses such violent images in describing the voice of the Lord? (David was trying to communicate the awesome, almost unfathomable power of God. To people who don't know God, such power might be as frightening as the natural disasters David described.)

7. Can you think of other less violent images in nature that God's voice might be compared to? If so, what are they? How do those images make you feel about God?

8. Psalm 29:10 says that the Lord "sits enthroned over the flood." What do you think David is talking about

here? (David may be referring to the flood during Noah's day. The point he's trying to make is that nothing is beyond God's control—including natural disasters.)

9. **How could you use Psalm 29 to answer people who claim that all nature is God and God is all nature?** (Psalm 29 portrays God as having complete power over all nature. To suggest that all nature is God is to limit God.)

10. **After emphasizing the strength and might of the Lord, Psalm 29 concludes with the phrase, "The Lord blesses his people with peace"** (29:11). **Do you see any significance in that? Explain.** (It suggests that even though God is all-powerful, He is loving and can be approached as a friend.)

After focusing so heavily on God's power and might in Psalm 29, spend some time at the end of the session concentrating on God's other characteristics. Read Romans 11:33-36; then briefly discuss God's wisdom. Read I John 4:7-12; then briefly discuss God's love. Read I John 1:9; then briefly discuss God's faithfulness and forgiveness. Invite those who don't know God or His Son, Jesus Christ, to begin a personal relationship with this powerful, wise, loving, faithful, and forgiving Lord. Close the session in prayer, praising God for His power and might, as well as His other characteristics.

WHAT A DISASTER!

Match the following natural disasters with the correct clues. If you get all of them right, you'll receive a prize. So be careful—one little mistake could be disastrous.

a. Tornado
b. Hurricane
c. Earthquake
d. Avalanche
e. Volcanic eruption

____ 1. Touch down!

____ 2. The snowball effect

____ 3. Hugo

____ 4. Where's Pompeii?

____ 5. A 2.3 is much better than a 7.6.

____ 6. Caused by two plates rubbing together

____ 7. Frosty's nemesis

____ 8. Mr. Cold Front, meet Mr. Warm Front.

____ 9. A calm eye

____ 10. Bye, bye, Dorothy!

____ 11. Nickname for the University of Miami's sports teams

____ 12. Let's play Twister!

____ 13. Catch a wave

____ 14. Whose fault is it?

____ 15. Prehistoric lava lamps

PSALM 37

Don't Worry, Be Righteous

David pleads with the Israelites to be blameless before God and not to long for the "quick fix" rewards of sin, because a lasting reward from God awaits those who are righteous.

(Needed: Prizes)

Hand out copies of the reproducible sheet, "A Quick Quiz." After several kids have begun the sheet, announce that you will accept only kids' *first* responses—no one may change an answer. Then give some "missing" instructions for the quiz. For #1: **Misspell your answer.** For #2: **Write your answer as small as possible.** For #3: **Print your answer.** For #4: **Write your answer in cursive.** For #5: **Write your answer upside down.** For #6: **Write your answer in the bottom left corner of the sheet.** For #7: **Write your answer so that it slants downward.** Award prizes to the first three kids to hand you their quizzes with the answers written correctly. (The answers are as follows: [1] John; [2] Ohio; [3] basketball; [4] North America; [5] 8; [6] Steven Spielberg; [7] *The Simpsons.*) Use the activity to introduce Psalm 37:7.

DATE I USED THIS SESSION _____ GROUP I USED IT WITH _____

NOTES FOR NEXT TIME _____

_____

_____

1. What kinds of things do you think most people your age are envious of? What kinds of things make you envious? How do you react when you're envious? How do you treat people you're envious of?

2. Why might Christians be envious of people who do wrong (37:1)? (Some Christians may feel "constrained" by living a Christian life. They may feel that people who do as they please, without worrying about pleasing God, have a better time in life.)

3. Read through Psalm 37. **What are some of the characteristics of wicked people?** (They scheme [37:7]; they plot against righteousness [37:12]; they use violence and threats to overcome "upright" people [37:14]; they do not repay their debts [37:21]; they "lie in wait" for righteous people [37:32].)

4. What are some of the characteristics of righteous people? (They trust in the Lord [37:3, 5]; they are humble [37:11]; they give generously [37:21, 26]; they are peaceable [37:37].)

5. What do you think Psalm 37:2 means when it says that people who do wrong will "wither" and "die away" like plants? (The apparent success of evil people will eventually shrivel up and amount to nothing.)

6. What is the promise we have from God in Psalm 37:4 if we stay committed to Him? (He will give us the desires of our heart.) Does this mean that the Lord will give us anything we want? Explain. (If we're committed to the Lord and delight in Him, the desires of our heart will be in accordance with His will. So when God's will is done, He will be giving us the desires of our heart.)

7. Why is it sometimes difficult to "wait patiently" for the Lord—especially when we see wicked people succeeding all around us (37:7)?

8. How hard would it be for you to convince your friends that Psalm 37:16, 17 is true? Why? What would you say to try to convince your friends of the truth of this principle?

9. Why is the Lord's promise to Christians in Psalm 37:23, 24 so reassuring? (We know that the Lord is always watching over us and will pick us up when we fall.) **In what situations of your life might this promise be especially meaningful? Explain.**

10. Do you think it's more difficult for Christians today to stand strong and resist the temptation to envy people who do wrong than it was for righteous people in David's time? Explain.

(Needed: Party supplies)

David makes the point in Psalm 37 that we shouldn't envy wicked people who seem to be succeeding and having a good time because eventually those people will be destroyed and the righteous will prevail. But for many young people, the idea of postponed gratification isn't very appealing. Help your group members see that being a Christian doesn't mean giving up all fun and enjoyment until we get to heaven. Throw a party! Bring in your group members' favorite snacks. Play some of their favorite games. Celebrate the fact that Christians can succeed in having just as much fun as non-Christians do. [NOTE: If you don't have time for a party at the end of your session, take a few minutes to plan a party for sometime within the next couple of weeks.]

A QUICK QUIZ

The first three people to correctly complete this quiz and hand it to the group leader will receive a prize. If you think you can answer the following questions correctly on your own, you may begin; if not, you may want to wait for your group leader to offer some helpful hints.

1. Who wrote the Book of John in the New Testament?

2. What state is round on both ends and "hi" in the middle?

3. What sport allows the least amount of traveling?

4. On what continent would you find the United States?

5. In bowling, if you have a 7-10 split left, how many pins did you knock down on your first ball?

6. Name the person who directed *Jaws*, *Jurassic Park*, and *Schindler's List*.

7. What TV show features characters named Krusty, Mr. Burns, Barney, and Lisa?

PSALM 42

Desire Under Fire

In Psalm 42, which is written as a song, the sons of Korah cry out to God, using poetic language to describe their desire for Him. Even though the psalmists are being persecuted and taunted by their foes, they continue to put their hope in God and praise Him.

(Needed: Prizes; a recording of "Desire" by U2 and a tape player [optional])

Hand out copies of the reproducible sheet, "How Badly Do You Want It?" Encourage group members to be as creative and humorous (while still being tasteful) as possible in their responses. Announce that you will award prizes for the most creative response to each statement. Give group members a few minutes to work. While kids work, you might want to play the song "Desire" by U2 (from the album *Achtung Baby*). After everyone is finished, go through the statements on the sheet one at a time, asking group members to call out their responses. Vote as a group on which response is most creative; then award prizes accordingly. Use the activity to introduce Psalm 42, in which the psalmists vividly and poetically describe how desperately they long for God.

DATE I USED THIS SESSION _____ GROUP I USED IT WITH _____

NOTES FOR NEXT TIME _____

_____

_____

1. What one thing in your life have you desired more than anything else? Have you ever gotten something that you really desired? If so, what was it like?

2. How might outside problems—such as persecution from others—affect a person's desire for God? How did persecution affect the psalmist's desire for God (42:3-6)? (Some people may allow outside problems to shift their focus away from God. The psalmist, however, turned to God even more passionately when he was faced with persecution.)

3. Compare Psalm 42:5, 6 with James 1:2, 3. How are the two passages similar? How are they different? (Both passages emphasize the importance of turning to God and maintaining an optimistic outlook in the face of persecution. But James 1:2, 3 gives a reason for thinking of persecution as "pure joy"—persecution develops perseverance.)

4. Do you think it's possible to be "downcast," but still have your "hope in God" (42:5)? Explain.

5. What are some circumstances that can drag us down even when we know we have God on our side? (Being betrayed by a friend; worrying about things like money, clothes, and social status; etc.)

6. What do you think the psalmist is talking about when he says, "Waves and breakers have swept over me" (42:7)? (It's likely that psalmist was experiencing great distress, with wave after wave of trouble and sorrow rolling over him.) **Have you ever felt way? If so, what were the circumstances? What happened?**

7. If you had to choose one hymn or Christian song to keep with you all of the time (42:8), what would it be? What is it about that song that is so meaningful to you?

8. Do you think God ever forgets about His people (42:9)? Why does it sometimes seem that way? Do you think God is offended when people ask Him why He has forgotten about them? Explain.

9. **What does Psalm 42:11 tell you about the life of a Christian?** (Being a Christian may not always be easy or enjoyable. Sometimes God allows us to be tested to see how much we look to Him for strength and guidance.)

10. **On a scale of one to ten—with one being "not very hard at all" and ten being "nearly impossible"—how hard is it for you to praise God when things in your life are going really wrong? Explain.**

Hand out paper and pencils. Give group members an opportunity to create an analogy similar to the one in Psalm 42:1 to describe how intensely they seek God and His will. Do they "pant" for God in the same way that a deer pants for water? If so, they should come up with an updated version of that analogy. If their desire for God is a little less intense, they should come up with an analogy to reflect that (for example, "My soul longs for God like a car longs for an oil change— every three months or so"). After a few minutes, ask volunteers to share their analogies. Close the session in prayer, asking God to help your group members develop an intense desire for Him.

HOW **Badly** DO YOU **Want** IT?

We've all had things that we really wanted in life, right? Sure, no big deal. But have you ever *longed* for something? Like to the point where you were willing to donate a part of your body to science—right at that moment? Fill in each of the following scenarios with the most extreme, outrageous, wacky, humorous response you can possibly think of—without getting offensive or overly disgusting, please.

1. *I'm so hungry I could . . .*

2. *For just one date with the person of my dreams, I would . . .*

3. *If I could be assured of passing tomorrow's biology test, I would be willing to . . .*

4. *I would do anything to get rid of this headache—even . . .*

5. *If my dad would let me use the car on Friday night, I'd be willing to . . .*

PSALM 49

Poor Rich People

Psalm 49, written by the Sons of Korah, focuses on the folly of people who put their trust in wealth. The psalmists affirm the truth of the statement, "You can't take it with you," by pointing out that wealth cannot save someone from death. Only God can do that. Therefore, it's senseless for people who don't have wealth to be envious of people who do.

(Needed: Dice, play money, a nice prize)

Hand out a copy of the reproducible sheet, "The Money Game," and some play money to each person. Make sure everyone has the same amount of money (perhaps $100) in the same denominations (perhaps a $50 bill, a $20 bill, two $10 bills, a $5 bill, and five $1 dollar bills). Allow kids to read the instructions on the sheet, but don't elaborate on the rules of the game at all. Have kids sit in a circle. One at a time, have each person roll the dice and follow the appropriate instructions on the sheet. Periodically during the game, hold up the prize that kids are playing for—perhaps a gift certificate for a nice clothing store or restaurant—as incentive. Play 3-5 rounds. Afterward, announce that the person with the *least* amount of money left is the winner and award the prize. Lead in to a discussion of Psalm 49.

DATE I USED THIS SESSION _____ GROUP I USED IT WITH _____

NOTES FOR NEXT TIME _____

_____

_____

1. Imagine that you're participating in a debate. The topic of the debate is "Resolved: Money can't buy happiness." What three points would you use to argue *for* this statement? What three points would you use to argue *against* this statement?

2. Be honest here: Do you believe that money can buy happiness? If so, in what circumstances? If not, why not?

3. If you could get the attention of the entire world for five minutes—perhaps via a global satellite hookup—what would you say? Why? Note the introduction to Psalm 49 in verses 1-4. Then compare group members' responses with the words of the psalmist in Psalm 49:5-20.

4. What might cause a person to trust in his or her wealth? What's so bad about trusting in wealth? Explain. See Luke 16:13. (People who build fortunes have a tendency to be self-reliant and proud; people who inherit fortunes have a tendency to view themselves as privileged. Either way, their identities are built on their wealth. Jesus says that no one can "serve" money and God.)

5. How would you explain Psalm 49:7-9 to a non-Christian friend who comes from a wealthy family?

6. How "costly" is "the ransom for a life" (49:8)? See Matthew 20:28; John 3:16; and Romans 3:23-26. (Jesus paid the ultimate price—He took the sins of the world upon Himself, suffered the agony of physical torture and separation from God, and gave His life to pay the "ransom" for our lives.)

7. It seems kind of obvious to say that wealthy people are as likely to die as poor people are. What point do you think Psalm 49:10-12 is trying to make? (Ultimately, it's pointless to spend one's life pursuing wealth, because when a person dies, his or her wealth is useless to him or her.)

8. Why do you think people have a tendency to be "over-awed" by wealth and obvious riches (49:16)? What's the problem with being captivated by the wealth of others?

9. Do you think it's possible for a person to have riches *with* understanding (49:20)? Explain.

10. Compared to people in the rest of the world, how wealthy would you say you are? Explain.

11. Based on Psalm 49, what advice would you give to a wealthy person? Explain.

(Needed: Chalkboard and chalk or newsprint and marker)

As a group, discuss what it means to "trust in wealth." Come up with some guidelines concerning what does and doesn't constitute trusting in wealth. Ask: **How much emphasis should we place on money? How should we use the money we have? How can we prevent ourselves from trusting in wealth?** Write group members' responses on the board. Then pare down the list to the top ten suggestions. Hand out paper and pencils. Give group members an opportunity to copy the list. Ask them to post it in a place where they will see it often, as a reminder of the dangers of trusting in wealth.

$ THE MONEY GAME $

To play "The Money Game," roll the dice and follow the appropriate instructions (according to the number you roll). Keep in mind that the winner of the game will receive a great prize—so roll carefully.

 —Give $1 to every other player.

 —Collect $15 from the player on your right.

 —Trade stacks of money with the player on your left.

 —Collect one bill of any denomination from the player on your left.

 —Trade stacks of money with the player who has the least amount of money.

 —Trade stacks of money with the player of your choice.

 —Give one bill of any denomination to the player on your right.

 —Collect $5 from every other player.

 —Do not collect any money; do not give any money away.

 —Give $10 to the person on your left.

 —Give away all but $5 of your money to the player of your choice.

PSALM 51

Oh, Mercy!

The story of David's affair with Bathsheba is recorded in II Samuel 11–12. After David is confronted by the prophet Nathan, he composes this great psalm of repentance. The psalm, which moves from confession to praise, starts from an inward, personal focus and moves to an outward focus, with David pleading for the entire nation. David demonstrates what real confession is all about—sincerely desiring to turn from wrong and trusting in the unfailing love of God.

(Needed: Stained fabric, stain-treating agents, sink)

Before the session, put a number of stains on some type of fabric, using things like permanent marker, catsup, dirt, and grape juice. Keep the stains separate. Bring in some stain-treating agents (club soda, soap, Wisk, lemon juice, etc.). Begin the session near a sink. Divide into teams and give each team an identical set of stains and cleansing agents. See which team can do the best job of removing the stains in five minutes. Afterward, ask: **How is getting rid of sin like and unlike getting rid of stains?** Talk about some of the ways in which people try to get rid of guilt. Point out that only God can get us completely clean. Then read through Psalm 51, paying particular attention to verses 2 and 7.

DATE I USED THIS SESSION _____ GROUP I USED IT WITH _____

NOTES FOR NEXT TIME _____

_____

_____

Q&A

1. What's the dirtiest you've ever been in your life? How did you get dirty? How long did you stay dirty? How did it feel to clean up?

2. The introduction to Psalm 51 mentions how David came to write the psalm. What actually happened between him and Bathsheba? Review the events in II Samuel 11–12, noting the nature of David's sin, his denial of it, and the consequences of it.

3. How does it make you feel to know that this event is in the Bible? (It shows how human David was. It gives us hope that God can forgive our sins.)

4. Which of the characteristics of God mentioned in Psalm 51:1-9 are most meaningful to you? Explain. (Several characteristics are mentioned—including God's mercy; His unfailing love; His compassion; and His roles as judge, teacher, and crusher of bones.)

5. David says he's only sinned against God (51:4). What does David seem to mean by this? Does David's statement seem to ignore the effect that sin has on other people? Explain. (Even though other people were hurt by David's sin, it was ultimately a violation of God's law.)

6. Some people say that human beings are basically good. What do you think David would say about that (51:5)? (He's aware that he's always been a sinner—it's his natural predisposition.)

7. What do you think David's talking about when he mentions the "inner parts" (51:6)? (It's the core of his being, his most secret place. Many people hide their deepest, darkest sins there. God wants to bring the light of His truth to these "dark closets.")

8. David makes a number of requests in Psalm 51:7-15. Which requests do you have questions about? Why didn't David just say, "Forgive me" and leave it at that? (His request goes beyond forgiveness—he also wants to restore the joyful relationship with God he once had. Note how his sin was keeping him from praising God.)

9. **Why does God take delight in a broken spirit** (51:16, 17)**? Does He get some sort of satisfaction out of our pain?** (A broken spirit refers more to the realization that we can't make it on our own without God. It acknowledges our total dependence on Him. He takes delight in us when we are truly humble before Him.)

10. **How is the ending of Psalm 51 different from the beginning** (51:18, 19)**?** (David shifts his focus from himself to his nation. Sometimes it's easy to get totally self-absorbed. This psalm is a reminder that there are issues beyond ourselves that we need to be concerned about.)

11. **What are some of the different motivations people might have for confessing their sins to God? Based on Psalm 51, what do you think the** *primary* **motivation should be?** (Some motives might include wanting a clear conscience, getting rid of guilty feelings, wanting to go to heaven, wanting to escape hell, etc. Maybe the primary motivation should be that it's the natural response to the unfailing love God has for us [Psalm 51:1]. Another key motivation is wanting to restore the most important relationship we have.)

The obvious application of Psalm 51 is to give group members an opportunity to confess their own sins to God. This is something that can't be forced, so be sensitive to your group members' current condition. The reproducible sheet, "True Confessions," might help group members focus their thoughts. Give kids time to work on the sheet individually. Read through some of the other psalms of penitence (6, 32, 38, 102, 130, 143) as a group or have kids skim them silently. When everyone is finished, ask volunteers to share the verses that were most meaningful to them. Afterward, as a group, discuss some of the effects that guilt has on us. Then close with a time for silent prayers of confession, followed by prayers of thanksgiving. Group members might want to read back to God what they've written on the sheet for section #4.

True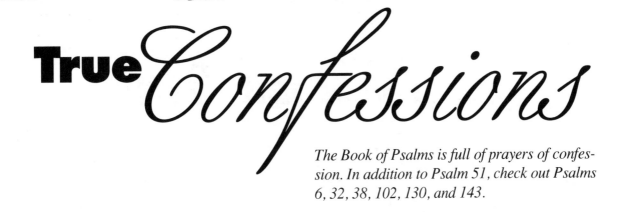

The Book of Psalms is full of prayers of confession. In addition to Psalm 51, check out Psalms 6, 32, 38, 102, 130, and 143.

1. From these psalms, select one or two verses that are most meaningful to you right now.

2. These psalms talk a lot about the effects of guilt. Finish this sentence: "When I feel guilty, I . . ."

3. God wants you to "come clean" with Him. He already knows everything there is to know about you, so confessing your deepest, darkest sins is for your own benefit. Shade in the heart below to symbolize how pure or impure your heart is right now. If your heart is 100% pure, don't mark it up at all. If you have a little bit of sin to confess, shade in a little bit. If you have some big time sins to confess, shade in more. Keep this between you and God—no one else needs to see your paper.

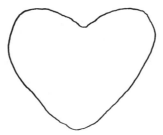

4. Write a prayer of thanksgiving below in response to the unfailing love and great compassion God has for you.

Lord, thank You for Your . . .

PSALM 63

Thirst and Goal

Psalm 63, a relatively short psalm of David, starts off with words of intense longing and thirsting for God and ends with the certainty that those who are truly committed to God will rejoice and praise Him, while all enemies (liars) will finally be put in their place. It was written when David was hiding from his enemies in the Desert of Judah, so it's no wonder that David was thirsty!

(Needed: Thirst-causing food items, beverages)

Bring in an assortment of food items guaranteed to make your kids thirsty—popcorn, pretzels, beef jerky, etc. Let group members eat, but keep all liquid refreshment off limits. You might want to display the beverage, but forbid kids from drinking it. Have group members form two teams. Give each team a copy of the reproducible sheet, "I'm Thirsty." One team should make a list of words that people associate with thirst—parched, dry, hot, etc. The other team should make a list of words that sound refreshing—splash, oasis, liquid, etc. See which team can create the longest list in two minutes. Let the winning team enjoy something to drink, but keep the "losers" thirsty a while longer.

DATE I USED THIS SESSION _____ GROUP I USED IT WITH _____

NOTES FOR NEXT TIME _____

_____

_____

1. What's the thirstiest you've ever been? What were you doing that made you so thirsty? How long did you thirst? What did you eventually drink? Describe how it felt to drink it. After this discussion, let your "losers" from the Opening Act have something to drink.

2. Why do you think David was in the desert (introduction to Psalm 63)? (Many Bible scholars think this refers to the time when David was hiding from his own son, Absalom, who wanted to kill him. [See II Samuel 15–17.]) **How was this desert experience affecting David's relationship with God** (63:1, 2)? (David felt distant from God. He probably missed worshiping God in the sanctuary. His physical thirst probably reminded him of his even greater thirst for God.)

3. Describe a time when you felt really distant from God. What was it like? How did you deal with it?

4. Considering that his own son—and many others—were trying to kill him, David probably had a lot to worry about. With that in mind, how would you describe the general tone of this psalm (63:3-11)? What word or words are repeated several times? (The overall tone is very hopeful. The word "will" is repeated eleven times. David seems to know that God "will" take care of him.) **What's David looking forward to?** (Being able to praise God, having his hunger satisfied, being delivered from his enemies, etc.)

5. What percentage of the people that you know do you think would agree with David's statement in Psalm 63:3 that God's love is better than life? If people really felt this way, how would it affect the way they live their lives?

6. What words would you use to describe David's relationship with God? How do you think he and God got to be so close? (God seems to be the most important thing in David's life. Notice the tense shift from future to present in Psalm 63:6-8. As David looks forward to many things, he recognizes that God is his helper here and now too.)

7. What do you suppose David means when he says, "I sing in the shadow of your wings" (63:7)? (It's two images of God's protection in one. A shadow protects people from the heat of the sun and the wing of a mother bird protects baby birds from harm. In the same way, God protects those who put their trust in Him.)

8. **In Matthew 5:44, Jesus tells His followers to love their enemies. Do you think David loved his enemies** (63:9-11)? (Even though David was certain that his enemies would get their "just reward" in the end, he left the timing up to God. This was a pattern throughout his life. Early on, he had two chances to kill King Saul, but didn't. Now, he could have done away with Absalom, but chose not to. The behavior of his enemies saddened him, and David felt real grief when Absalom died.)

9. **What does it mean to "swear by God's name"** (63:11)? (It certainly *doesn't* mean cussing, and it also doesn't mean simply using His name when taking an oath, like swearing on a stack of Bibles. It refers to those who purposely live their lives to honor God and trust Him.)

10. **How do you think your relationship with God compares to David's? How thirsty for God are you?**

(Needed: Poster board, marker)

As a group, make a list of things that are good about life—good friends, family, great food, etc. Hand a piece of poster board and a marker to one group member and have him or her write something down. Then have the person pass the poster board and marker to the next person, who will write down something else. Keep going until you have twenty or more things on the list. Then review the list, affirming just how good life is. Read Psalm 63:3 several times, substituting each of the things on the list for the word "life." For example, "Because your love is better than *good friends,* my lips will glorify you." Have each group member participate in this litany. Close the session by using your lips to glorify God—through song, prayers of praise, or by praying portions of Scripture to God that talk about how great He is.

I'm Thirsty

Thirsty Words

Refreshing Words

PSALM 68

Our God Is an Awesome God

Psalm 68 is a celebration of God's rule over His people. It evokes images of God's presence with His chosen ones, leading them in a joyful procession. It refers to God's progression from Mount Sinai in the days of Moses to Mount Zion in the days of David, where He established His throne in the temple in Jerusalem.

(Needed: An assortment of items, a paper bag)

Bring in several small items—a spoon, an eraser, a credit card, a chess piece, etc. Place one of the items in a paper bag. Let a volunteer feel the item in the bag. The volunteer's goal is to get other kids to guess what's in the bag using as few clues as possible. At first, the volunteer may only describe how the item *feels*. If no one guesses it, the volunteer may describe how the item *looks*. If kids still haven't guessed it, the volunteer may describe *what the item is used for*. Play other rounds as time allows. Afterward, discuss how it's even more difficult to describe God in words. Point out that Psalm 68 uses a lot of imagery to describe the Lord.

DATE I USED THIS SESSION _____ GROUP I USED IT WITH _____

NOTES FOR NEXT TIME _____

_____

_____

1. Have you ever been in a parade? If so, what kind of parade was it? Why were you in it? How did it feel to be in it? How did you feel about parades as a kid? What did you enjoy most about them? What didn't you like? Point out that Psalm 68 talks about a very different type of parade, with God leading the way.

2. Read through Psalm 68. Make a list of the words used to describe God—strong wind, fire, one who rides on the clouds, a father, defender, song leader, provider for the poor, etc. **Which of these images mean the most to you? Why?**

3. Psalm 68:1-3 is also descriptive of something else. What is being referred to in these verses? Here's a hint: read Numbers 10:33-35. (The psalmist describes the beginning of a triumphal procession of God's people, led by God, from Mount Sinai to Jerusalem in the promised land.)

4. In the first three verses of Psalm 68, David pleads with God to lead and watch over His people amidst their enemies. Has there been a time in your life when you felt and knew that God was "clearing the way before you" and watching over your life? If so, explain.

5. What types of people does God seem to especially care about in Psalm 68:5-10? Why is this? How have you seen this to be true? (God has special concern for orphans, widows, poor people—those who especially need His loving care in their lives. His concern is to set lonely people in families where they can be loved. For many, this is the church family. God also cares about those who are prisoners—this probably refers to the Israelites being held captive in Egypt.)

6. What in the world is Psalm 68:11-18 talking about? (It probably refers to the taking of the promised land by the Israelites. Verses 17 and 18 are key—they speak of God choosing to dwell in His sanctuary in Jerusalem.)

7. How does God daily bear our burdens (68:19)? (This could refer to a number of things—taking our burdens to God in prayer, God's removing the burdens of enemy nations, and God's ultimately removing the burden of sin and death.)

8. **What's going on in Psalm 68:28-31?** (The psalmist is pleading that God would continue to protect His people in the land of promise. Enemies still threatened God's people when this psalm was written. The "beast among the reeds" probably refers to the Pharaoh in Egypt—a symbol of all powerful enemies. The "herd of bulls among the calves of the nations" probably symbolizes either princes in Egypt who served Pharaoh or to other enemy nations that weren't as powerful as Egypt.)

9. **Which view do you think this psalm supports—that God is just the God of Israel or the God of all nations?** (God chose to begin His work in Israel, but it's clear that all of the kingdoms of the earth will eventually praise Him [68:32].)

10. **In what ways is God awesome** (68:35)? **What does the word "awesome" mean, anyway?**

Hand out copies of the reproducible sheet, "God-in-a-Box." The sheet lists several misconceptions people have about God. Have kids form groups. Assign one or more of the misconceptions on the sheet to each group. Instruct each group to answer the three questions on the sheet about its assigned misconception(s). After a few minutes, have each group share its responses. Then, as a group, discuss why people sometimes try to understand God in human terms to make Him more manageable. In reality, He's much bigger, much more powerful, much more awesome, much more mysterious than we can imagine. Ask which view of God your kids think is most common and which views they are most likely to hold. Challenge group members to think about the "boxes" they keep God in and pray that He might expand their boxes this week.

Psalm 68:35 says that God is "awesome." The word "awesome" has lost some of its meaning lately. It means "inspiring profound and humbly fearful reverence." It means that no matter how hard we try, we'll never completely figure God out. Below are some faulty views people have of God. For each view, answer these three questions:
• Why might someone hold this view of God?
• How might people live their lives if they held this view of God?
• What Scripture verses support or contradict this view?

1. The Cosmic Killjoy
God doesn't want people to have any fun. All He cares about are rules.

2. The Generous Genie
God is ready to grant our every wish.

3. The Supernatural Sheriff
God's making a list, checking it twice. He's going to find out who's naughty or nice.

4. The Old Man Upstairs
God created the world and all, but now He's just letting it run its own course.

5. The Busy Businessman
God's too busy to be concerned with my trivial concerns.

6. The Perfectionist
I can never be quite good enough to please God.

PSALM 73

Standing on Shaky Ground

Psalm 73, a psalm of Asaph (one of David's choir leaders), deals with God's goodness to those who trust in Him. It focuses on the temptation to envy those who don't trust in God, especially when it seems that they're getting away with murder.

(Needed: Two carpet squares, two pillows)

Begin the session by simulating the joust event from the *American Gladiators* TV show. Ask for two volunteers. Place two carpet squares on the floor about two feet apart. The volunteers should stand on the squares facing each other. Give each volunteer a pillow. At your signal, volunteers will try to knock their opponent off the square using only the pillow. Each match should last no more than thirty seconds. The first person to successfully knock his or her opponent off the square wins the round. Play until you think kids have had enough. Try to redeem the activity by pointing out that Psalm 73 talks about losing your foothold and about people who stand on slippery ground.

DATE I USED THIS SESSION _____ GROUP I USED IT WITH _____

NOTES FOR NEXT TIME _____

_____

_____

1. Tell about a time when you slipped or fell down. What were you doing? Why did you slip? Did anyone see you fall? If so, how did that person react?

2. Read Psalm 73. **If the psalmist were writing these words today, where might he have been while writing them? What kind of people might he have been watching? Who was he envying?** (Maybe he was in some place where bodies were on display and people were obviously proud of themselves and their evil deeds. Sounds like he could have been in a locker room, or at the beach, or at a party.)

3. **What did the psalmist envy about these arrogant and wicked people?** (Their bodies, their freedom to do as they please, their lack of problems, being carefree, their wealth.) **Which of these things do you think Christians today are most likely to envy in others? Why?**

4. **Describe what it's like to envy someone. What types of thoughts go through your mind? What effects, if any, do your envious feelings have on your life—your self esteem, your relationships, your faith?** (Envy always takes a toll. It might cause us to think less of ourselves—and less of God.)

5. **What are some things about the people described in Psalm 73 that aren't enviable?** (Their pride, their violence, their callousness, their arrogance, their speech, their flippant attitudes about God, their "final destiny.")

6. **What's the psalmist feeling in Psalm 73:13, 14? When have you felt that way?** (When he sees the fun that the arrogant people are having, he questions his own lot in life. Maybe he felt the discipline needed to follow God wasn't worth the price.)

7. **Why does the psalmist's perspective change in Psalm 73:17?** (It wasn't until he entered God's sanctuary that he saw things from God's perspective.) **How does your perspective of life change when you're aware of God's presence?**

8. **How did the psalmist's perspective change?** (Before, he envied the wicked people; now he sees that their days are numbered. Their earthly pleasures are very temporary. In comparison to the great privilege of knowing God, and in the scope of eternity, these people are missing out on what really matters.)

9. **In what ways does God help the psalmist out?** (God holds him up, guides him, has a future of glory planned for him, etc.)

10. **What clues can you find in Psalm 73 about the psalmist's priorities?** (Psalm 73:25, 28 makes it very clear that the psalmist's relationship with God was more important than anything else.)

11. **If someone asked you to tell of God's deeds in your life (73:28), what are some of the deeds you'd list? Explain.**

(Needed: Chalkboard and chalk or newsprint and marker)

Write the following letters on the board: A, E, F, H, and I. Ask: **What other letters belong in this series?** (The correct answer is as follows: K, L, M, N, T, V, W, X, Y, and Z.) Hand out copies of the reproducible sheet, "JEALOUS E," which will help explain the sequence—it's all of the straight letters of the alphabet. Give group members a few minutes to figure out what the story is saying, asking them to uncover the moral of the story. Here's what the story says after the letters switched places: "So, E changed places with O and you can guess what happened next—A switched places with S and pretty soon, the whole alphabet was a total mess! So, the moral of the story is this: Don't envy what others have—God made you the way you are for a very good reason." Afterward, say: **Some people accuse Christians of being straight, or square. Are they? Why are many Christians viewed this way? What are the costs of being a Christian? What are some of the benefits? Is it worth it to follow Jesus? What can you do the next time you're feeling envious of those who don't put their trust in God?**

JEALOUS *E*

ONCE UPON A TIME, THERE LIVED A LETTER. HIS NAME WAS E. E WAS AN IMPORTANT LETTER, USED IN A LOT OF WORDS. ONE DAY, E LOOKED AT HIMSELF IN THE MIRROR AND SAID, "I'M KIND OF A SQUARE. MY RELATIVES, A, H, I, K, L, M, N, T, V, W, X, Y, AND Z ARE ALL SO STRAIGHT! I'D GIVE ANYTHING TO BE LIKE THOSE WILD LETTERS—B, C, D, G, O, P, Q, R, S, AND U. THEY'RE SO MUCH MORE EXCITING." SO E CHANGED PLACES WITH O AND YEU CAN GUOSS WHAT HAPPONOD NOXT—A SWITCHOD PLACOS WITH S SND PROTTY AEEN, THO WHELO SLPHSBOT WSA S TETSL MOAA! AE, THO MERSL EF THO ATERY IA THIA: DEN'T ONVY WHST ETHORA HSVO—GED MSDO YEU THO WSY YEU SRO FER S VORY GEED ROSAEN!

PSALM 78

He Forgives and We Forget

Psalm 78 emphasizes the importance of passing on God's teachings and recounting His deeds from generation to generation. The psalm traces the many things God did for His people after rescuing them from Egypt. Time after time, God showed the people mercy and forgiveness, only to see them rebel. They would be punished and would turn back to Him. God would forgive and the people would forget. The psalm concludes with a reference to the great shepherd-king, David, and foreshadows the ultimate reign of Jesus, the son of David.

Quickly read the following ten answers, but don't let anyone write them down: **969; Jedidiah; 1,189; Isaiah; I Chronicles 1:25; Esther; 46,227; Gomer; II Kings** (6:29)**; Absalom.** Then distribute copies of the reproducible sheet, "This Is a Test." Since you just gave away the answers, allow only one minute for kids to complete the sheet. Afterward, see how many answers your kids remembered. Explain that Psalm 78 addresses the tendency people have to forget what God has done for them. Point out that the psalm also refers to "tests" three different times.

DATE I USED THIS SESSION _____ GROUP I USED IT WITH _____

NOTES FOR NEXT TIME _____

_____

_____

1. Tell about a time you forgot something really important. What was it you forgot? What were the consequences?

2. Explain that you're going to read a lengthy psalm; to help group members pay attention, they must perform various hand motions anytime they hear certain words or phrases. **Any time you hear a reference to anger, make a fist. Any time you hear a reference to remembering or forgetting, point to your head. Any time you hear a reference to the heart, point to your heart. Any time you hear a reference to speech or talking, point to your mouth. Any time you hear a reference to hearing, point to your ears. Any time you hear a reference to a test, throw both of your hands up in a panic.** Practice a few times; then read Psalm 78. **What struck you as we read through this psalm?**

3. **What are some of the things mentioned in this psalm that God has done for His people throughout Israel's history?** Make a list on the board. **Which events are most amazing to you?**

4. **Why is it so important to pass these stories on from generation to generation (78:3-8)?**

5. **Why are people so prone to forgetting what God has done for them (78:9-33)?** (The "men of Ephraim" [78:9] refers to the northern kingdom [Israel] that was much more rebellious than the southern kingdom [Judah]. Note the connection between the people's forgetfulness and their willful disobedience. It's as if people purposefully forget about God so they can live their lives as they please.)

6. **What does it mean to "put God to the test" (78:18, 41, 56)?** See Exodus 15:22-25; 16:1-4; 17:1-4. (God was testing the people's ability to trust in Him, but they repeatedly failed the test. They were putting God's patience to the test through their grumbling, disobedience, and lack of trust in Him.)

7. **What are some ways you put God to the test? When is it hardest for you to trust Him? When is it hardest for you to be obedient?**

8. **What does Psalm 78:32-39 say about human nature and God's nature?** (People have ample proof of God's existence, but choose to rebel against Him. When hard times come, they turn to Him. God continually shows that He is forgiving, slow to anger, and abounding in love.)

9. **How could God be so loving** (78:38, 52, 68) **yet so angry** (78:21, 31, 58, 59)**?** (We need to keep both characteristics of God in balance—His unfailing love and His perfect holiness which can't tolerate any sin. God is love—and He's perfectly holy. His anger burns against all things that keep people from experiencing His love.)

10. **Why did God love David so much** (78:68-72)**?** (David was a "man after [God's] own heart" [I Samuel 13:14; Acts 13:22]. God seems to have a soft spot in His heart for "shepherds," as He Himself is the Great Shepherd. Even though David messed up big time more than once, his repentance was sincere—his heart was in the right place. He had integrity of heart. Also, God chose David's tribe [Judah] to be the tribe from which the Messiah—Jesus, the Son of David—would come.)

(Needed: Concordances or study Bibles)

Spend some more time talking about God's love and His holiness. Have kids form two groups. Give each group a concordance or study Bible. Have one group find Scripture passages to support the fact that God is a loving, compassionate, slow-to-anger father. Have the other group find passages to support the fact that God is a holy, righteous, angry, jealous judge. After a few minutes, have the groups share the passages they found. Ask: **What would a person's life be like if he or she only thought about God's love? What would a person's life be like if he or she only thought about God's holiness or His anger? Do you think most church people's view of God is out of balance? If so, how? Is your view of God out of balance in either direction? If so, how can you achieve a better balance?**

THIS IS A Test

This is a test. For the next sixty seconds, we will test to see how well you remember the answers that were so generously given a moment ago. Had this been a real test (like the S.A.T. or A.C.T. or G.M.A.T. or P.S.A.T. or the dreaded J.E.S.T.), you would have real cause for panic. But luckily for you this is just a test. And if you keep reading this pointless introduction, you'll totally forget the correct answers and your sixty seconds will be over. Who said church is no fun? Who comes up with this stuff, anyway? What kind of sick minds are at work here? We can't believe you're still reading this! Now take the test. Umm, we said take the test. Did you hear us? Hello, is anyone home? We now resume our regularly scheduled programming. This was only a test.

1. How many years did Methusaleh live?

2. What was Solomon's other name?

3. How many chapters are in the Bible?

4. Who walked around naked for three years?

5. What's the shortest verse in the Old Testament?

6. What's the only book of the Bible that doesn't mention God?

7. How many times does the word "and" appear in the Bible?

8. God told Hosea to marry a prostitute named _____.

9. In what book do we find a woman who boiled and ate her son?

10. Who got his head caught in a tree while riding a mule?

PSALM 84

Templesick

Psalm 84 is a beautiful psalm of longing for God's presence. It has a lot in common with another psalm "of the Sons of Korah"—Psalm 42. Psalm 84 focuses on the psalmist's longing to be in the Lord's dwelling place—His temple in Jerusalem. The psalmist was probably a Levite who used to be very involved in worship at the temple. He was probably in captivity and full of melancholy about the "good old days." Yet, the psalm shows great faith in God's goodness. Even though he's full of sorrow, the psalmist considers himself blessed.

Hand out copies of the reproducible sheet, "Wishful Thinking." Give group members a few minutes to write down their thoughts and draw a picture in the thought balloon. Afterward, ask volunteers to share what they wrote and drew. Then say: **Let's take a look at a psalm written by a guy who might have been a prisoner in a foreign land.** Read Psalm 84 together. Compare the psalmist's feelings with the types of things your group members wrote. Ask: **How are your feelings similar to and different from the psalmist's?** See if any of your group members say they would miss church.

DATE I USED THIS SESSION _____ GROUP I USED IT WITH _____

NOTES FOR NEXT TIME _____

_____

_____

Q&A

1. When have you been the most homesick? Why were you so homesick? How long did it last? How did you get over it?

2. How do your views about church differ from the psalmist's? Why do you think the psalmist missed God's "dwelling place" (84:1) so much?

3. Does God really dwell in a building? Can't we worship Him anywhere? Explain. (Obviously, God isn't confined to any one location, but in Old Testament times, the temple in Jerusalem was the symbol of His presence on earth. When Jesus was crucified, the curtain in the temple was torn, symbolizing that God's Spirit would now take up residence in the hearts of people, not in a physical temple.)

4. Who does the psalmist consider to be envied (84:3-5)? Who do you consider to be enviable? (The psalmist envied the sparrows who had nests near the temple. He also considered temple dwellers fortunate. This may refer to priests and others who assist in temple worship. He also considered all those whose strength was in God to be blessed. He probably included himself in this category. Even though he couldn't physically be in the temple courts, his heart could journey there.)

5. What is this Valley of Baca, anyway (84:6)? (It probably refers to any type of dry, arid place. The name may mean "weeping.")

6. The psalmist begs God to hear and listen to him (84:8). Do you think there are times when God doesn't hear our prayers? See Isaiah 1:15. (When our prayers are just for show or when we have unconfessed sins or a proud spirit, God will not listen.)

7. What's the psalmist asking for in Psalm 84:8-11? (He's asking for protection for the king in Jerusalem. It's possible that the city was under siege by an enemy nation at this time and that's why the psalmist couldn't get to the temple. If the psalmist's king prospered, then free access to the temple might be restored.)

8. Do you really believe that God doesn't withhold any good thing from those whose walk is blameless (84:11)? Why or why not? Or is it a moot point, since no one is blameless anyway? (Abraham was called "blameless" in Genesis 17:1 and we know he sinned from time to time. But his life was evidenced by obedience to God and trust in God's faithfulness. When discussing "good things," make a list of the "good things" God gives us. These are often different from the "good things" people selfishly want.)

9. Why is someone who trusts in God considered blessed (84:12)? What are some ways that God has blessed your life?

10. What words would you use to describe the overall tone of this psalm? (Even though the psalmist is sad, he shows great faith in God.)

Even though God no longer "dwells" in the temple or in any particular church building, one fitting application of Psalm 84 is to discuss how kids in your group feel about your church. Have your group members rate on a scale of one to ten the following areas of the church:
• How meaningful are the worship services?
• How real are the people?
• How inspiring is the music?

As a group, make a list of the things about the church that cause people to complain. Then talk about why people complain about these things. Afterward, affirm the importance of meeting together with others to worship God and the need to weed out hypocrisy and avoid empty forms of worship. But keep in mind that what's "empty" to one person may be "meaningful" to another, depending on his or her current heart condition toward God.

Wishful Thinking

Suppose you're a prisoner of war in a far-off land. You've been away from your homeland—and all of the things that you love about it—for a long, long time. You realize that you may not ever return home. One day, you're sitting around with a lot of time on your hands, and you start to think back to the good old days. You get out your journal and start writing down some of your thoughts.

1. What do you miss most? (Draw a picture of the most lovely thing you can think of in the thought balloon above.)

2. What places do you have the fondest memories of?

3. What people back in the homeland do you consider to be the most fortunate? What are they doing right now?

4. What are you thinking about God right now?

5. You're starting to feel a little poetic. How would you complete the following sentences? (Don't worry, they don't have to rhyme.)

Better is one day in _____

Than a thousand in _____ ;

I would rather be a _____

Than a _____ .

PSALM 86

Someone's Praying, Lord

Psalm 86, a psalm of David, describes what it's like to trust God—even when enemies are making life difficult. It's not clear from the psalm if these enemies are people inside the kingdom or outside. Whatever the case, these arrogant people were attacking the psalmist in some way—perhaps verbally, perhaps physically. The psalm serves as a good model of a prayer that balances requests and praise.

(Needed: Sheets of paper prepared according to instructions)

Before the session, write each word from the following children's bedtime prayer on a separate sheet of paper: "Now I lay me down to sleep; I pray the Lord my soul to keep. If I should die before I wake, I pray the Lord my soul to take." Scramble the sheets; then see how long it takes your group to assemble the prayer in the correct order. If kids aren't familiar with the rhyme, they'll have to guess at it. Afterward, ask: **What's good about this prayer? How is it weak? How does it compare to your own prayers?** Explain that in this session, you'll be looking at a prayer in the psalms.

DATE I USED THIS SESSION _____ GROUP I USED IT WITH _____

NOTES FOR NEXT TIME _____

_____

_____

1. Hand out copies of the untitled reproducible sheet. **Pretend this scroll was just discovered in a cave in Israel. It's the only piece of Scripture you've ever seen. Follow the instructions on the sheet, trying to discover as much as you can about this ancient document.** The sheet contains the complete text from Psalm 86 in the New International Version. Let kids work on it individually or in small groups. After about ten or fifteen minutes, discuss it together. **How did you title the psalm? What words did you circle or underline? What else did you notice about it? What questions did you come up with?**

2. **Scholars think that David wrote Psalm 86 when he was king. If so, how could he be poor and needy (86:1)?** (Often in Scripture, the word "poor" has less to do with material wealth than it does with people's recognition that they are powerless to save themselves and are therefore totally dependent on God. This is what Jesus apparently meant by "poor in spirit" in Matthew 5:3.)

3. **David says he calls on God all day long (86:3)? How is that possible? How often do you call on God?** (David may be referring to an awareness of God's presence with him all of the time. This might be what Paul meant by praying continually in I Thessalonians 5:17.)

4. **When do you think people pray the most? When do you pray the most?** (Perhaps in times of trouble [86:7], when a loved one is sick, when confronted with the beauty of nature, etc.)

5. **Psalm 86:8 mentions many gods. Isn't God the only one? What does the psalmist mean here?** (Perhaps the psalmist is referring to the idols of surrounding nations. In Psalm 86:10, he affirms that God alone is God.)

6. **What gods—or things—compete for God's attention in your life? Why?**

7. **What do you think it means to have an "undivided heart" (86:11)?** (Matthew 6:21 says, "For where your treasure is, there your heart will be also." Maybe having an undivided heart means treasuring your relationship with God so much that nothing else even comes close when it comes to what's really important in life.)

8. **Has God ever delivered you "from the depths of the grave"** (86:13)? **If so, how?** If no one mentions it, point out that this is exactly what Jesus has done for us.

9. **Why does the psalmist ask for a sign** (86:17)? (To shame his enemies.) **What signs does God give to unbelieving people today?** (Creation, the love of Christians, a sense of right and wrong, etc.)

10. **How does the prayer of the psalmist in Psalm 86 compare to most of the prayers you offer to God?**

As you wrap up the session, focus on what real prayer is. Skim through the Book of Psalms, looking for examples of prayers of adoration, confession, thanksgiving, and supplication (requests). Ask: **Which type of prayer do you offer most? Why?** Also spend some time discussing the two-way nature of prayer—it's much more than simply talking *at* God. Discuss how God communicates to people today. How do we "hear His voice" amidst the "noise" of life? Come up with a list of specific suggestions for improving one's prayer life. Challenge each group member to choose one or two of the suggestions to practice this week. Close with a time of prayer, focusing on adoration, confession, thanksgiving, and supplication.

Title _____

A prayer of David.

Hear, O Lord, and answer me, for I am poor and needy.

Guard my life, for I am devoted to you. You are my God; save your
   servant who trusts in you.

Have mercy on me, O Lord, for I call to you all day long.

Bring joy to your servant, for to you, O Lord, I lift up my soul.

You are forgiving and good, O Lord, abounding in love to all who call
   to you.

Hear my prayer, O Lord; listen to my cry for mercy.

In the day of my trouble I will call to you, for you will answer me.

Among the gods there is none like you, O Lord; no deeds can compare
   with yours.

All the nations you have made will come and worship before you,
    O Lord; they will bring glory to your name.

For you are great and do marvelous deeds; you alone are God.

Teach me your way, O Lord, and I will walk in your truth; give me an
   undivided heart, that I may fear your name.

I will praise you, O Lord my God, with all my heart; I will glorify your
   name forever.

For great is your love toward me; you have delivered me from the
   depths of the grave.

The arrogant are attacking me, O God; a band of ruthless men seeks
   my life—men without regard for you.

But you, O Lord, are a compassionate and gracious God, slow to anger,
   abounding in love and faithfulness.

Turn to me and have mercy on me; grant your strength to your servant
   and save the son of your maidservant.

Give me a sign of your goodness, that my enemies may see it and be
   put to shame, for you, O Lord, have helped me and comforted me.

INSTRUCTIONS
1. Give the prayer a title.
2. Circle all of the requests the psalmist is making.
3. Underline all of the words that describe what God is like.
4. Connect words that seem to be repeated multiple times.
5. List any questions you have about the passage.

PSALM 90

Moses Knows Us

Psalm 90, attributed to Moses, deals with the shortness of life. In many ways, Psalm 90 is similar to the themes expressed in the Book of Ecclesiastes, which state that life without God is pretty meaningless. This psalm concludes with Moses' plea to God to show His splendor to future generations and to help the "work of our hands" have some lasting significance.

(Needed: Prizes)

Have kids form teams to complete the reproducible sheet, "Who Lives Longer?" When a team is finished, check its answers and announce how many are correct. Then let the team try again. After the second round, award prizes to the team that gets the most correct. The correct answers are as follows (from shortest life to longest life): mayfly; housefly; worker bee; shrew; house mouse; queen bee; walleyed pike; queen termite; dog; cat; emperor penguin; human tapeworm; boa constrictor; hippopotamus; gorilla; American alligator; Indian elephant; human being; quahog clam; black Seychelles tortoise. Afterward, say: **Psalm 90 says that most people live between seventy and eighty years (90:10)—which is true. In the scope of eternity, seventy or eighty years isn't very long. That's what Psalm 90 talks about.**

DATE I USED THIS SESSION _____ GROUP I USED IT WITH _____

NOTES FOR NEXT TIME _____

_____

_____

1. What do you think would be the best age to die? Why?

2. Who wrote the Book of Psalms? (Most people would probably answer David. He wrote many of them, but Psalm 90 was written by Moses!)

3. Read through Psalm 90. **How does this psalm make you feel? What parts seem kind of depressing? Which verse is most depressing? What parts seem kind of hopeful? Which verse is most hopeful?**

4. **What does it mean that God has been the people's dwelling place** (90:1)**?** (He's been their protector, their refuge.)

5. **Psalm 90 doesn't make much mention of any sort of afterlife. Why do you think that is?** (Moses knew a lot less about God's plans for us than we do. God has revealed much more about the afterlife since Moses lived.)

6. **What does it mean to "number our days aright"** (90:12)**?** (Maybe it means we need to keep in mind how short our life on earth really is. This gives us a much wiser perspective on life.)

7. **Do you think most people in this country number their days aright? What evidence is there to support your answer?**

8. **What seems odd to you about Psalm 90:15?** (The concept of being glad and afflicted at the same time is a bit strange. Discuss whether or not this is possible.) **Read James 1:2, 3. Does this passage make Moses' statement in Psalm 90:15 any clearer? Explain.**

9. **Most people want their life to have some lasting significance. In what ways can your life make a difference after you're dead** (90:16, 17)**?** (We can pass on a legacy to future generations. The things we do—"the work of our hands"—can be established.)

10. What "works of your hands" do you want to be around after you're gone?

There's something in all of us that wants to live on after we die. Some people call this our soul. If there isn't any God, then after seventy or eighty years, it's all over. How do your kids feel about this? Ask: **What hope do we have that there really is such a thing as eternity?** Reread Psalm 90:1, 2. Then ask: **What difference does it make to you that God is "from everlasting to everlasting"?** Let kids think about this some. Do they all have a trusting relationship with this everlasting God? Do they understand how Jesus makes it possible for us to enter into a relationship with Him? Is there any hope in life apart from Him? These are deep, but important questions. Make yourself available to meet one on one with those who aren't certain about these things. Close with some words of hope from the New Testament, like Romans 8:31-39 or II Corinthians 4:16-18.

WHO LIVES Longer?

Put the following animals in order from the one that lives the shortest amount of time to the one that lives the longest—based on the longest recorded life span for each animal.*

American alligator	**Human being**
Black Seychelles tortoise	**Human tapeworm**
Boa constrictor	**Indian elephant**
Cat	**Mayfly**
Dog	**Quahog clam**
Emperor penguin	**Queen bee**
Gorilla	**Queen termite**
Hippopotamus	**Shrew**
House mouse	**Walleyed pike**
Housefly	**Worker bee**

1 day _____

2 months _____

6 months _____

18 months _____

3 years _____

6 years _____

18 years _____

25 years _____

27 years _____

31 years _____

34 years _____

35 years _____

40 years _____

43 years _____

49 years _____

56 years _____

69 years _____

113 years _____

149 years _____

152 years _____

* Based on the book, Why Does a Turtle Live Longer than a Dog? by Barbara Ford (William Morrow and Company, 1980). Human being maximum age is based on modern records, not biblical accounts.

PSALM 91

Gimme Shelter

Psalm 91 speaks simply and directly of the protection of God and the security He brings to a godly person. It reminds us of the promise of victory when enemies attack. It also assures us that if we make God our dwelling place, then He makes us His dwelling place!

(Needed: Some kind of "projection" device; a white bedsheet [optional])

Bring in either a filmstrip projector, a slide projector, or a big flashlight. Start the session by having group members cast their favorite hand shadows on the wall (providing, of course, that none of the shadows are offensive). The rest of the group will try to guess what the hand shadows are representing. Another option is to have group members act out a particular Bible story from behind a white bedsheet with a light shining from behind them. Ask one group member to read the Bible story while others act out—using their shadows—what's being read. Afterward, hand out copies of the reproducible sheet, "Only the Shadow Knows." After a few minutes, have volunteers display what they came up with. Use the activity to introduce the idea that there is a shadow—the "shadow of the Almighty"—that knows all about us.

DATE I USED THIS SESSION _____ GROUP I USED IT WITH _____

NOTES FOR NEXT TIME _____

_____

_____

1. What's the worst or most unusual place you've ever had to sleep or take shelter in? Explain.

2. What does the word "shelter" make you think of? What about the word "refuge"? What kinds of things serve as shelters or refuges for you?

3. From what does God protect us, according to Psalm 91:3-13? What meaning do you give to these disasters? (The fowler's snare, deadly pestilence, the terror of the night, flying arrows, plagues, the wicked, the lion, the cobra and the serpent are all things that represent evil, sin, death, and dangers in life.) **What attitude should we have toward evil, according to the psalmist (91:5, 7-10)?** (We should remain confident, not fearful.)

4. What is the requirement for receiving God's protection (91:9, 10)? (Taking refuge in Him; *asking* Him for protection.)

5. What are some things we use to protect and secure valuables? (Locks, safes, ropes, etc.) **What does God use to protect us?** (Angels; His own power.) **If God is protecting us, why do bad things happen to Christians?** (Sometimes people choose to leave the protective "umbrella" God provides. In other situations, God allows us to face difficulties in order to strengthen us.)

6. How does God show favor to those who love Him (91:14-16)? (Deliverance, protection, answers to prayer, divine presence, long life, satisfaction, salvation.)

7. What can we learn about angels from this psalm?

8. Do you think you really have guardian angels watching over you? If so, describe what you imagine them to be like. How do you suppose they protect and take care of you?

9. Compare Psalm 91:9 with John 15:4-7. **What does it mean to make God our dwelling place? Based on the**

branches-and-vine analogy, why is it important for us to dwell in God?

10. **What can we learn about God from Psalm 91:14-16? Explain.** (God rescues us because of our love for Him. Acknowledging His name is important to God. God's protection and "coverage" is comprehensive.)

(Needed: Tape player and tape; video player and video [optional])

Bring in a tape of Amy Grant's song "Angels Watching Over Me" from her *Straight Ahead* album. Play the song (or show the video, if possible). Afterward, have group members make a list of fears and troubles they have in their lives for which they want God's protection and deliverance. Then ask: **What is your part in this process?** Encourage group members to "do their part" by maintaining things like regular devotions/Bible study and prayer time. Emphasize that these things make us feel closer to God and His protection.

If you can't locate the Amy Grant album, try another option. Have kids form teams. Have a contest to see which team can come up with the most songs, TV shows, movies, phrases, or anything else that have something to do with angels (angel fish, angel hair pasta, *Charlie's Angels,* the California Angels, etc.). Afterward, contrast the biblical view of angels with the secular view of them.

ONLY THE SHADOW KNOWS

What if our shadows showed what we were really thinking or feeling? What if they showed what was really going on in a situation? What kinds of things might they show? Take a look at the following pictures; then draw shadows to indicate what *really* might be going on.

PSALM 96

Glory Be

OVERVIEW

Psalms 96–99 are frequently classified as psalms of the "enthronement of the Lord." These hymns of praise are sung to the kingship of God. In Psalm 96, the psalmist gives three admonitions: sing to the Lord, give to the Lord, and look for the Lord's return.

OPENING ACT

Hand out copies of the reproducible sheet, "Top Ten." Let group members work in pairs or small groups to complete the top half of the sheet, "The Ten Best Excuses for Not Going to Church." (Save the bottom half for later in the session.) Encourage them to be as creative and humorous (though non-offensive) as possible. After a few minutes, have each pair or small group share its list. Then vote as a group on the best excuses from each list to come up with a top ten list for the entire group. Afterward, point out that church attendance is something a lot of people struggle with. Explain that in this session, you'll be talking about the importance of corporate worship.

DATE I USED THIS SESSION _____ GROUP I USED IT WITH _____

NOTES FOR NEXT TIME _____

_____

_____

1. If somebody asked you why Christians go to church every week, what would you say? How do you feel about going to church every week? Do you enjoy it? Do you do it out of obligation? Or do you blow it off? Explain.

2. In Psalm 96, the psalmist lists several things that are to be included in the worship of God. What are they? (Singing, proclaiming salvation, ascribing glory to God, declaring His deeds, bringing an offering, rejoicing, etc.) **Are there any other things you think should be included in worship? If so, what?**

3. What is your favorite hymn? How about your favorite praise chorus? Why?

4. What do you think the psalmist means when he says that the Lord "is to be feared" (96:4)? How does a person show fear of the Lord with a sense of joy and excitement? (To fear the Lord means to show the respect and honor due Him.)

5. How do you think bad habits and unconfessed sin affect a person's worship of God? Explain.

6. Psalm 96:9 speaks of trembling before God, which is another reference to having a fearful, reverent awe before God? When is the last time you've "trembled" before God? How did you feel after that experience?

7. Psalm 96:10 states that "the Lord reigns"; but I Peter 5:8 says that "the devil prowls around . . . looking for someone to devour." If the Lord reigns over the world, why do you think He allows Satan to have so much power?

8. Psalm 96:10-13 indicates that God's judgment should be an occasion for rejoicing. Why do we often view God's judgment with dread rather than as the psalmist does?

9. The last part of Psalm 96 is prophetic in announcing the coming of the Lord. The psalmist talks positively about the event, as though looking forward to the day. But how do you think most of the world will view God's day of judgment? Why?

10. **What kinds of things make worship experiences meaningless and boring to some people? What are some things that** can be done to change this?

Have kids return to the groups they formed in the "Opening Act." Instruct them to complete the bottom half of the sheet ("The Top Ten Best Things about Going to Church"). After a few minutes, have each group share its list. Then, if you have time, design as a group a worship service that would be creative and meaningful for your group members. You might want to assign different areas of a worship service to different groups to work on. For example, you might have a music group, a Scripture and prayer team, a celebration committee, etc. Write down each group's suggestions. Consider taking them to your pastor or church board for possible implementation in a future service.

The Top Ten Best Excuses for *Not* Going to Church | **The Top Ten Best Things about Going to Church**

1.

2.

3.

4.

5.

6.

7.

8.

9.

10.

PSALM 100

Glad to Be of Service

Psalm 100, a psalm of thankful praise, concludes the "homage psalms" (95–100). It was sung by the people as they approached the gates of the temple to offer sacrifices of thanksgiving. It includes seven commands that make up the formula for overcoming ingratitude and for living joyfully.

Hand out copies of the reproducible sheet, "Joy-o-Meter." Explain that this is a test to measure group members' joyfulness. Give kids a few minutes to complete the sheet. Afterward, explain that Psalm 100 is intended to help us consider our attitudes of joy and gratitude toward God for creating us and being continually faithful to us, even when we stray from Him.

DATE I USED THIS SESSION _____ GROUP I USED IT WITH _____

NOTES FOR NEXT TIME _____

_____

_____

1. Name seven things that you're thankful for. How do you show your thankfulness?

2. What reasons does the psalmist give for praising God (100:5)? (The Lord is good; His love endures forever; He is faithful.)

3. What are some of the commands listed in Psalm 100? (Shout joyfully, gladly serve, know Him, enter His gates with thanksgiving and praise, give thanks, praise His name.) **Which of these commands is most difficult for you? Why?**

4. What attitudes should characterize God's people, according to Psalm 100? (Thankfulness and joyfulness.) **On a scale of one to ten, how joyful are most Christians? How joyful are most parents? How joyful are most teenagers?**

5. Why do you think some Christians seem to be so solemn, serious, or even negative? How might a person fall into such a frame of mind? How can we change that? How do you express joy?

6. What is the opposite of thankfulness? (Apathy or ingratitude.) **What are some signs of gratefulness?**

7. One evidence of true worship and service is an attitude of gladness. How "contagious" is an attitude of gladness? Explain.

8. What do passages like Colossians 3:23; Romans 12:1, 2; and Matthew 25:40 have in common with Psalm 100? (Serving others springs from a joyful, thankful heart.) **How might serving others make a person more grateful or joyful?**

9. If enthusiasm, thankfulness, and joy can make such a big difference in life, what can you do to incorporate these things in your life? How can we make our church a more joyful place?

10. How do you feel about the statement, "You become like the people you hang around"? Name an enthusiastic,

positive person you know and explain how that person's attitude has helped you.

On the back of the reproducible sheet, have group members list two or three people that they are grateful for. Then, as a group, brainstorm some creative ways to express gratitude to those people in the coming week. The ideas don't have to be expensive or complicated—they might involve things like writing a note of encouragement, giving a small gift, washing a person's car, mowing a lawn, etc. As you wrap up the session, emphasize the importance—and life-changing potential—of joyful service.

Joy-o-Meter

Answer the following questions by circling the appropriate answer. Be honest, please. Then shade in the "joy-o-meter" based on the number of "yes" answers you circled. If, when you're finished, you don't like the level that your joy-o-meter is at, check out the listed verses for each area in which you circled a "no" response.

YES   NO   1. Do you usually avoid criticizing people you don't like? (Romans 14:13)

YES   NO   2. Do you rejoice always? (Philippians 4:4)

YES   NO   3. Do you avoid putdowns, usually giving encouraging words? (Colossians 4:6)

YES   NO   4. Have you thanked the Lord for anything today? (Colossians 3:15-17)

YES   NO   5. Do you rarely grumble or complain when you're asked to do something? (Philippians 2:14)

YES   NO   6. Do you regularly say "thank you"? (I Thessalonians 5:18)

YES   NO   7. Are you a positive person, excited about what the Lord is doing in your life? (Romans 12:11)

YES   NO   8. Do you usually show your appreciation for others? (Romans 15:2)

YES   NO   9. Do you say positive things about your enemies? (I Peter 3:9)

YES   NO   10. Do you bring cheer and laughter wherever you are? (Proverbs 17:22)

YES   NO   11. Do you thank God for the food you eat? (John 6:11)

YES   NO   12. Do you thank God when He answers your prayers? (John 11:41)

PSALM 103

Thundershowers of Blessings

Psalm 103 is part of a collection of hymns used for public worship. It's a praise song to the Lord of creation and the Lord of history. It is attributed to David, and is thought to have been written in his old age, summarizing God's dealings with him. Unlike many other psalms attributed to David, Psalm 103 is a corporate praise hymn rather than a personal prayer of thanksgiving.

(Needed: Prizes)

Hand out copies of the reproducible sheet, "Perks Plus." Let group members work in pairs to complete the crossword puzzle. Award prizes to the first pair who correctly completes it. (The correct answers are as follows: *Across*—[1] forgiveness; [2] citizenship; [3] benefits; [4] friends; [5] love; [6] joy; *Down*—[1] peace; [2] salvation; [3] guidance; [4] spirit; [5] freedom; [6] purpose.) Afterward, ask: **What's so great about being a Christian?** Use the ensuing discussion to lead in to a study of Psalm 103.

DATE I USED THIS SESSION _____ GROUP I USED IT WITH _____

NOTES FOR NEXT TIME _____

_____

_____

1. If you were trying to describe the most enormous thing you can think of, what words would you use? What if you were trying to describe it poetically? What if you were trying to describe it humorously?

2. What are some of the benefits of a relationship with God that are mentioned in Psalm 103? (Forgiveness for sins, healing of diseases, redemption, love, compassion, youthful vigor, justice, etc.) **Rank these benefits according to how important they are to you. Explain your rankings.**

3. What does David mean in Psalm 103:4 when he says that God redeems lives "from the pit"? (God rescues people from the grave by providing eternal life through his Son.)

4. Compare Psalm 103:5 with Isaiah 40:31. **What does it mean to have your youth renewed like an eagle's?** (Perhaps it refers to a revived spirit, a newfound energy, a positive outlook on life, etc.)

5. If "the Lord works righteousness and justice for all the oppressed" (103:6), **why do oppressed people still have problems?** (The Lord works according to *His* timetable. Although we may not know *when,* we can rest assured that God will eventually bring about justice for the oppressed. Of course, none of us can expect many of God's benefits apart from commitment to Him.)

6. Do you think the Lord still makes His ways known to people today (103:7)? If so, how? If not, why not?

7. Why doesn't the Lord "treat us as our sins deserve or repay us according to our iniquities" (103:10)? (Romans 6:23 tells us that the wages of sin is death, but the gift of God is eternal life in Jesus Christ our Lord. It is Christ's sacrifice that allows us to receive God's grace.)

8. In Psalm 103:11-13, David makes several comparisons regarding God and His love for and mercy on us. Which comparison do you like best? Why?

9. Without using words like "good" or "secure," describe how Psalm 103:19 makes you feel.

10. Why is it important to praise the Lord?

11. If a person knew nothing about God, what could he or she learn about Him from Psalm 103?

Close the session with a time of silent prayer. Encourage your group members not to *ask* the Lord for anything during their prayers, but simply to praise God for who He is and what He's done in their lives. Give kids an opportunity to read through Psalm 103 again before the prayer time, so that they might use David's words as a model for their prayers.

PERKS PLUS

Being a Christian and obeying the Lord bring with them some wonderful blessings or "perks." We've included some of these blessings in this crossword puzzle. If you can't figure out an answer from the given clue(s), look up the accompanying Bible verse. Good luck!

ACROSS

1. Something you should give others if you expect to receive it yourself; Ephesians 1:7.

2. Anyone wishing to become president of the United States must have an American _____; Philippians 3:20.

3. When you get a job, these might include medical insurance, life insurance, and stock ownership options; Psalm 103:2.

4. One of Michael W. Smith's most popular songs; John 15:14.

5. A "many-splendored thing"; more pop songs have been written about this topic than any other; II Timothy 1:7.

6. The first word in a famous Christmas carol; can also be used as a girl's name; John 15:11.

DOWN

1. The "gentler" half of Leo Tolstoy's most famous book; John 14:27.

2. One of the world's most famous—and most musical— armies; Acts 4:12.

3. Many high schools have this type of counseling available to students; Proverbs 1:5.

4. Good cheerleaders possess a lot of this; I Corinthians 5:5.

5. This allows an American citizen to say whatever he or she likes; it's also what most prisoners crave; II Corinthians 3:17.

6. A reason for being; "You did that on _____!"; Philippians 2:2.

PSALM 119

Industrial Light and Lamp

OVERVIEW

Psalm 119, the longest psalm in the Bible, reflects on the Word of God. It is written in the form of a song. The psalm is divided into twenty-two sections of eight verses each. The title of each section is a letter of the Hebrew alphabet, and each verse in that section, if read in the original language, starts with that same letter. This type of poetry is called acrostic. The song of praise in Psalm 119 provides an alphabet of prayers and reflections on the Word of God.

OPENING ACT

(Needed: Prize)

Distribute copies of the reproducible sheet, "Lost in Maze" face down. Don't let group members look at the sheet yet. Explain that when you say, **Go,** group members should turn the sheet over and work through the maze as quickly as possible. The first person to successfully work through the maze is the winner. Award a prize (perhaps a flashlight) to the winner. Afterward, explain that in this session, you're going to look at a psalm that describes how God's Word can "light our way" through the tough times in life.

DATE I USED THIS SESSION _____ GROUP I USED IT WITH _____

NOTES FOR NEXT TIME _____

_____

_____

1. What's the darkest place you've ever been in? What was it like? How did you feel? What was it like when you finally saw light again?

2. Point out that Psalm 119:105 is the basis for the classic Amy Grant song, "Thy Word" (from the album, *Straight Ahead*). If possible, play a portion of the song. **How does the Bible serve as a lamp to our feet and a light for our path? Have you ever used a portion of Scripture as a lamp or light? If so, explain. If not, why not?**

3. The word enthusiasm comes from the Greek roots *en theos,* which means having "God inside" or to be full of God. In other words, enthusiasm means God's presence in your life! What are some words in Psalm 119 that you would consider to be part of "enthusiasm"? (Delight, treasure, excitement, love, wonder, rejoice, etc.)

4. What things in life cause you to be enthusiastic? Why?

5. According to the psalmist, how does a person keep from sinning (119:9-11)? (By memorizing God's Word and applying it to life situations.) **How do you think this works? How has it worked in your own life?**

6. What do you think it means to delight in God's decrees or laws (119:16)?

7. Do you think there's a difference between simply obeying God's law and delighting in it? If so, what's the difference? Why do you think some people simply obey God's law, without delighting in it?

8. What are some of the benefits from delighting in God's law? (Freedom in Christ, insight, wisdom, eternal life, hope for the future, happiness.)

9. How do you think obeying God's laws and guidelines gives someone freedom (119:32, 45, 67, 96)? Doesn't it seem like a person would be restricted by all of the "dos and don'ts"? Explain.

10. Read Psalm 119:72, 127. **How valuable is God's law? If given the choice, which would you take: $1,000 or a good Bible study? Be honest. Then explain your answer.**

11. **Think of the many benefits of studying God's Word. Which one means the most to you? Why?**

Point out that Psalm 119 is an acrostic song, in which each section begins with a subsequent letter of the Hebrew alphabet. Give your group members an opportunity to create an acrostic psalm about God's Word using as many different letters as possible from the English alphabet to begin each line. Let kids work in small groups to complete the assignment. After several minutes, have each group share what it came up with. Close the session in prayer, thanking God for the light and lamp He's provided for us in His Word.

LOST IN MAZE

Help poor Mr. Struggling Christian find his way back to God's Word. He knows that it is a lamp for his feet and a light for his path, but he hasn't spent much time in it lately, and now he feels like his life is in the dark! Help him through the maze by drawing a line along the right path so that God's Word can help him out of the dark to see life a little clearer!

PSALM 121

Somebody's Watching Me

Psalm 121 is one of the "songs of ascents" (120–134). These songs were sung by Jewish "pilgrims" on their way to Jerusalem for the feasts. The emphasis of each of these songs is on trusting God no matter what and centering one's life on Him. Psalm 121 portrays God as the living helper who *never* sleeps, protecting us day and night.

Distribute copies of the reproducible sheet, "Wish You Were Here." For each incident on the sheet, have group members draw a picture that might appear on the front of a postcard from the site of the incident. Then have them write a brief message on the "back" of the postcard as though they're the character (or one of the characters) involved in the incident. After a few minutes, have volunteers share what they came up with. Afterward, point out that all of the situations involve God watching over His people. Then lead in to the study of Psalm 121.

DATE I USED THIS SESSION _____ GROUP I USED IT WITH _____

NOTES FOR NEXT TIME _____

_____

_____

1. What's the longest you've ever gone without sleep? What were the circumstances? How did you feel? How long did you sleep afterward?

2. When you need help with school problems, where do you turn? When you need help with family problems, where do you turn? When you have problems with a boyfriend or girlfriend, where do you turn? When you have problems with friends, where do you turn? What kind of help do you get from each of these sources?

3. Can you honestly echo the psalmist's words when he says, "My help comes from the Lord" (121:2)? If so, in what areas of life do you receive help from the Lord? If not, why not?

4. Why do you think the psalmist includes the phrase, "the Maker of heaven and earth," in describing the Lord (121:2)? (Perhaps the psalmist is showing that he's receiving help from the best source possible—the Creator of everything.)

5. Psalm 121:3 says that God "will not let your foot slip." So if someone "stumbles" or faces difficult situations, does that mean God isn't watching over him or her? Explain.

6. We know the Lord watches over Israel (121:4). What other people does the Lord watch over? Explain.

7. If God were applying for a job as your bodyguard, what credentials do you think He'd list on His resumé? (He works twenty-four hours a day, seven days a week, fifty-two weeks a year—He never takes vacations. He is all-knowing, so He's aware of the dangers that confront us—even when we aren't. He's all-powerful, so He can protect us from anything. He's perfect, so there's no need to worry about His calling in sick or showing up late for work.)

8. Without using words like "safe," "secure," or "good," how does it feel to know that God is watching over us all of the time?

9. **Is there a downside to having God watch over us all of the time? If so, what is it?** (Some people may say that if God watches over us all of the time, He'll see things that we may not want Him to see. However, that's part of His "protection plan"—He wants to protect us from sin and its consequences.)

10. **Describe a time when God protected you from something. Describe a time when you felt really secure in the Lord's care.**

Explain to your group members that while they may not have experiences as radical as the ones listed on the reproducible sheet, they still will have some scary times in their lives. Ask kids to come up with a list of situations in which they really need to be aware of God's constant watching over them. Perhaps it's at the biggest party of the year, where nearly everyone's getting drunk. Perhaps it's when they're with friends who are using offensive language. Perhaps it's when a non-Christian asks them about Christianity. Close the session by thanking God for the assurance we can have, knowing that He is constantly watching over us.

Wish You Were Here

For each of the following biblical incidents, draw a picture that might appear on the front of a postcard from the site of the incident. Then write a brief message on the "back" of the postcard, describing what you might be thinking if you were the Bible character involved in the incident. The first one has been done for you.

Moses and the Israelites in the Wilderness (Numbers 11)

Ah Wilderness!

DAY 3,650—
NOTHING NEW TO REPORT. STILL WANDERING, WAITING TO GET INTO PROMISED LAND. PEOPLE REALLY GETTING ON MY NERVES. ALWAYS WHINING. DON'T KNOW IF I CAN TAKE THIRTY MORE YEARS OF THIS.
YOUR SON-IN-LAW,
Moses

TO:
JETHRO
DESERT
MIDIAN

David and Goliath (I Samuel 17)

The Fiery Furnace (Daniel 3)

Daniel in the Lion's Den (Daniel 6)

Jonah and the Great Fish (Jonah 1–2)

PSALM 139

Search Me

Psalm 139 is a hymn of David, often called the wise man's prayer because it recognizes that God is the answer to tough personal questions. The psalm shows God to be real, personal, and involved in human affairs. It is the concluding prayer of thanksgiving in a series of similar prayers by David, (135–139).

Begin the session with an activity called "Amazing People Tricks" (a variation of David Letterman's "Stupid Human Tricks"). Ask each of your group members to share with the rest of the group a hidden "talent"—some unusual, humorous trick or skill that he or she has developed. For instance, one person might give an unusual juggling exhibition. Another might walk on his or her hands across the room. Another might belch "Mary Had a Little Lamb." (You get the idea.) Afterward, ask: **What other talents or abilities do you have that you're proud of?** Use this discussion to introduce the topic of being "fearfully and wonderfully made" (Psalm 139:14).

DATE I USED THIS SESSION _____ GROUP I USED IT WITH _____

NOTES FOR NEXT TIME _____

_____

_____

1. Who is the one person in the world who knows you best? Why does this person know you so well? How does it feel to be known well by another person? Explain.

2. Compare that person's knowledge of you with David's description in Psalm 139:1-6 of how well God knows us. How do the two compare?

3. How does God's total knowledge of you make you feel? (Perhaps vulnerable or "transparent.") **How did David feel?** (Amazed, awestruck by the scope of God's knowledge.)

4. Is there such a thing as a "secret" sin? Explain. (If God sees, knows, and perceives everything we do [139:2-5], nothing can be kept secret from Him.) **Why do you think some people believe they can "get away" with certain sins?**

5. In Psalm 139:7, David asks, "Where can I go from your Spirit? Where can I flee from your presence?" Why might someone try to run away or hide from God? What's a better solution?

6. Some people use Psalm 139:13-16 to argue against abortion. What point do you think they might be trying to make? (Because God forms each of us in our mother's womb and ordains our days before we're born, pro-life advocates argue that abortion ends the lives of viable human beings with an ordained future awaiting them.) **Do you think this argument makes sense? Why or why not? What might a pro-life advocate and a pro-choice advocate say about this passage?**

7. How might Psalm 139:16 calm a person's fears concerning the future? (Even though we may not know what the future holds for us, we can rest assured in the fact that God does. And we can trust that He will guide us according to His will.)

8. What is David talking about in Psalm 139:17, 18? (God's "thoughts" are expressed in His works. David is affirming how overwhelming God's works are.) **Which of**

God's works are most "precious" to you? Explain. How do you show your admiration for God's work?

9. How might Psalm 139 be a helpful passage for a person who has low self-esteem or a poor self-image? (The fact that we are fearfully and wonderfully made indicates that God paid special attention to us when He created us. This should give us a sense of worth, knowing that we are somebody in God's eyes.)

10. Do you think David's attitude toward God's enemies (139:19-22) **is admirable? Why or why not?** Compare group members' responses with Jesus' words in Matthew 5:43-48.

11. What might prevent someone from praying David's words in Psalm 139:23, 24? (Some people don't want their thoughts and actions scrutinized by God—either out of shame or out of an unwillingness to change.)

Hand out copies of the reproducible sheet, "A Personalized Psalm." This sheet will help group members "customize" portions of Psalm 139 to fit their own situations. After a few minutes, ask volunteers to read the portions of their personalized psalms that they're comfortable sharing. (But do not *force* anyone to share.) Encourage group members to keep their sheets handy as a reminder of God's personal work in their lives.

A Personalized Psalm

O Lord, You know everything about me. You know things that even my closest friends don't know. For instance, You know that I'm secretly scared of

_____ .

You know that more than anything else, I enjoy _____

_____ .

You know the thoughts I've been struggling with lately about _____

_____ .

You know the problem I'm facing now with _____

_____ .

You know how depressed I get when _____

_____ .

You know all of these things about me because You created me. You formed me in my mother's womb. You gave me my _____

personality. You gave me talents such as _____

_____ .

I praise You because I am fearfully and wonderfully made.

PSALM 141

The Original Bodyguard

Psalms 140–143 are all prayers for protection. In Psalm 141, David specifically prays for God to protect him from his desire to sin, to compromise, and to be unfaithful. David points out the many obstacles to his loyalty to God, and asks the Lord in quiet faith for victory. But David understands that this victory won't be easy. He prays for protection, for strength to withstand temptation, and for victory over evil and its desires.

(Needed: Prizes [optional])

Hand out copies of the reproducible sheet, "What's Missing?" Encourage group members to be creative as they braisntorm various protective items. After a few minutes, have group members share what they came up with. You might want to award prizes to the people who come up with the most protective items for each situation. Afterward, lead in to a discussion of the protection that the Lord offers us—the protection requested by David in Psalm 141.

DATE I USED THIS SESSION _____ GROUP I USED IT WITH _____

NOTES FOR NEXT TIME _____

_____

_____

1. Have you or anybody you know ever been saved from serious injury or even death because of some kind of safety device like a seatbelt or an airbag? If so, what were the circumstances?

2. What body parts are mentioned in Psalm 141? (Hands, mouth, lips, heart, head, bones, eyes) **Why do you think these body parts are mentioned in David's prayer for protection from sin and temptation?** (Sin can affect and manifest itself in many different areas of the body. By specifically identifying potential "offenders" on his body, David is readying himself to fight temptation on those fronts.)

3. Where does David focus his attention to overcome temptation (141:1, 2)? (On the Lord.) **What are some of the less effective methods people use to try to overcome temptation on their own?**

4. What kinds of temptation are hardest for kids your age to overcome? Why? How might focusing on the Lord help a person overcome each of these extra-difficult temptations?

5. Why might a person need a "guard" over his or her mouth and a "watch" over his or her lips (141:3)? In other words, why is the tongue so difficult to control? What sin of the tongue is hardest for you to resist? Why?

6. True or false? It's possible for a Christian to be drawn to what is evil. Explain your answer.

7. In Psalm 141:4, David describes the wicked deeds of evildoers as "delicacies." **What point is he trying to get across here?** (Sin would never tempt us if it wasn't at all appealing. But sin *is* appealing. Even though it has terrible consequences, sin sometimes seems like great fun. However, that fun is only temporary.)

8. Psalm 141:5 talks about being able to take criticism and correction from other believers who are trying to hold you accountable. How do you handle criticism and correction from other Christians? Do you ever think of it as a way that God may be trying to protect you? Why or why not?

9. **What is David's general attitude toward those who tempt him with sin and evildoing** (141:6, 9, 10)**?** (He wants nothing to do with them. He asks that they become caught in the traps of sinful temptation.) **What is your general attitude toward those who tempt you to do wrong? Do you flee from evil? Or do you embrace it, thinking you're strong enough to fight it? Why?**

10. **What are some potential losses you might have to deal with if you choose to flee temptation instead of embracing it?** (You might lose a boyfriend or girlfriend if you choose to stay sexually pure. You might lose some "friends" if you choose not to go drinking with them.)

11. **Why do you think some people choose disobedience over obedience to God?** (Sometimes people don't mean to disobey; it's just that many temptations look appealing, causing people to start thinking of themselves and their own pleasure.)

Give your group members an opportunity to write their own prayers of protection to God on the back of their reproducible sheets. In these prayers, kids should ask God to protect from specific troubling situations they're currently facing. After everyone is finished, have kids form groups of three or four. Ask the members of each group to pray their prayers together. (If you don't think your kids would feel comfortable praying together, give them an opportunity to pray silently.) Close the session by praying for God's protection from sin and its effects.

What's Missing?

In each of the following pictures, draw as many items as you can think of that might be used as protection. For instance, in the picture of the football player, you might draw shoulder pads, a helmet, etc. In addition to drawing *actual* protective items, come up with some creative new ideas for protection. See how many protective items you can come up with for each picture.

PSALM 146

The Hallelujah Chorus

The last five psalms in the Book of Psalms are called the hallelujah songs—hymns of pure praise. Each one begins and ends with the phrase, "Praise the Lord." In Psalm 146, the focus is on personal praise. The psalmist declares his loyalty and love for the Lord, and then warns others not to put their hope and trust in men, who will fail them. The rest of the psalm is spent praising God for who He is and what He does for those who love Him.

(Needed: Index cards)

Hand out index cards and pencils. Instruct each person to write down an incident in which he or she had an encounter with somebody famous. If kids can't think of anyone famous they've encountered, have them write down the celebrity they would most like to meet and the circumstances under which they would like to meet him or her. After a few minutes, collect the cards and read them. As you do, kids will try to guess whose card it is. Use this activity to introduce the idea of having an encounter with the best "celebrity" of all—God.

DATE I USED THIS SESSION _____ GROUP I USED IT WITH _____

NOTES FOR NEXT TIME _____

_____

_____

1. How often do people praise you? What kinds of things do they praise you for? How do you usually react when people praise you? How does praise make you feel?

2. How often do you praise God? *How* do you praise God? What kinds of things do you praise God for? Compare group members' responses with the psalmist's words in Psalm 146:1, 2.

3. What might prevent a person from praising the Lord? (Unconfessed sin; selfishness; not having an understanding of what the Lord is doing; etc.)

4. Give some examples of people who "put [their] trust in princes [and] mortal men" (146:3). (Followers of cult leaders; followers of some televangelists; people who depend on the opinions of others when it comes to making moral choices.)

5. Have you ever put your trust—the kind of trust that should be reserved for God—in other people? If so, what happened?

6. What's the problem with putting your trust in mortal humans? (Mortal humans die and are unable to complete their plans. Mortal humans cannot save themselves, let alone others.)

7. In Psalm 146:5, 6, the psalmist praises God for His creation and His faithfulness. If you were writing a psalm right now, what two things would you praise God for? Why?

8. What does Psalm 146:7-9 tell us about the Lord? (He helps the "underdogs"—the people who are often overlooked in society.)

9. Can you identify with any of the categories of "underdogs" in Psalm 146:7-9? If so, which one(s)? If not, do you feel "left out"? Explain.

10. Do you think God needs our praise and worship? Do you think we need to praise and worship God? Explain.

11. If you were to make a regular habit of praising God for the things He does, how might it make a difference in your Christian life? Explain.

Hand out copies of the reproducible sheet, "Brushes with Greatness." After a few minutes, ask volunteers to share their responses to the first two sections on the sheet. Then have kids form groups of three or four. Instruct the members of each group to pray together, praising God for the things they listed on the third section of the reproducible sheet. Encourage group members to make a habit of praising God for the things He's done and is doing in their lives.

Brushes with GREATNESS

You're taking a trip on an airplane with your family. Due to a seating mix-up, you're seated in the first-class section while the rest of your family has to sit in the coach section. As you take your seat, you're amazed to discover that you've been seated next to your favorite actor or actress. It's a long trip, and your famous seatmate actually seems interested in talking to you. What three compliments would you give to the person to "break the ice"? What three questions would you ask the person?

COMPLIMENTS
1.

2.

3.

QUESTIONS
1.

2.

3.

On the return trip, you're once again seated in the first-class section. This time, you're stunned to find that you're sitting next to your favorite professional athlete. Surprisingly enough, this famous person also seems interested in talking to you. What three compliments would you give him or her to "break the ice"? What three questions would you ask him or her?

COMPLIMENTS
1.

2.

3.

QUESTIONS
1.

2.

3.

When you arrive home, you get the greatest surprise of all. As you're unpacking your suitcase, God suddenly appears in your room and asks you if you'd like to talk. Think about it— the Lord God, the Creator of all things, is in your room! What three things would you most like to praise Him for face-to-face? What three questions would you like to ask Him?

PRAISES
1.

2.

3.

QUESTIONS
1.

2.

3.

PSALM 150

Have Breath, Will Praise

OVERVIEW

Psalm 150 aptly closes the Book of Psalms with its building crescendo of excitement and intensity with each praise. The psalm implies that the whole universe is one great temple in which "everything that has breath" is summoned to praise the Lord. The focus is the praise offered by every creature—past, present, and future—together in harmony.

OPENING ACT

(Needed: Karaoke machine or radio/cassette player)

Announce that you're going to "audition" your kids to see which of them are "worthy" of praising God. Bring in a karaoke machine or a radio/cassette player for kids to sing along with. Explain that kids may sing solo or in groups, but that *everyone* has to perform. Encourage kids to have fun with this activity. As each act performs, pretend to critique the performance by jotting down notes. After everyone has performed, announce which kids are worthy of praising God—all of them! Point out that the only qualification for praising God is found in Psalm 150:6—"Let everything that has breath praise the Lord."

DATE I USED THIS SESSION _____ GROUP I USED IT WITH _____

NOTES FOR NEXT TIME _____

_____

_____

1. What's your favorite musical instrument? What is it about that instrument that you like?

2. Psalm 150 concludes the Book of Psalms. What message do you think the psalmist wants his readers to come away with? (The importance of praising God through corporate worship.)

3. Where should God be praised (150:1)? ("In his sanctuary" and "in his mighty heavens" may refer to places where corporate worship takes place—in Jewish temples, Christian churches, etc.)

4. Why should God be praised (150:2)? (God should be praised "for his acts of power" and "for his surpassing greatness." Two of God's greatest acts of power are creation and redemption.)

5. Psalm 150:3-5 lists several different musical instruments that can be used to praise God—including trumpets, harps, lyres, tambourines, stringed instruments, flutes, and cymbals. What other instruments would you like to see added to this list? Why?

6. If you could change the musical portion of our church's worship service, what would you do? Why? How do you think the congregation would respond to your changes? Explain.

7. Do you think there are any musical styles that *aren't* appropriate for praising God? For instance, do you think jazz music is appropriate for worship? What about heavy metal? Alternative music? Dance music? Rap? Explain your responses for each style.

8. How might dancing (150:4) be used to praise God? Do you think dancing has any place in church worship services? Why or why not?

9. On a scale of one to ten—with one being "completely inhibited" and ten being "completely uninhibited"—how inhibited would you say you are in your personal worship of God? How inhibited are you in your corporate worship of God in your church? Explain.

10. Why do you think churches differ so much in their opinions of what is "acceptable" or "appropriate" when it comes to praising God in a worship service?

11. How might corporate praise—worshiping with other people—benefit your walk with Christ? (When we see others praising God for His greatness to them, it may cause us to think about what God has done for us.)

(Needed: CD/cassette player and recordings of Christian worship songs [optional])

Hand out copies of the reproducible sheet, "Praise Him." Let kids work in pairs or small groups to complete the sheet. Encourage them to be creative in their lists. While group members work, you might want to play recordings of several different styles of worship songs. For instance, you might play songs of praise from Christian pop groups, rap artists, country bands, heavy metal groups, etc. After a few minutes, have each group share what it came up with. Have kids write down any worship ideas that they might like to try. Encourage your group members to make praise and worship a part of their lifestyle.

Praise Him

The word "praise" appears thirteen times in Psalm 150, suggesting several different ways to worship the Lord ("with the harp and lyre," "with tambourine and dancing," etc.). If you were to come up with a list of thirteen ways to praise God today, what might that list include? (Praise Him with a drum solo? Praise Him by making a music video? Praise Him by designing worship-based computer software?) Be creative.

1.

2.

3.

4.

5.

6.

7.

8.

9.

10.

11.

12.

13.

PROVERBS 1–4

Wise Up

The first four chapters of Proverbs establish the purpose of the book—to attain wisdom. These chapters contain warnings against rejecting wisdom, as well as explanations of the benefits of wisdom. The major theme of the book is effectively captured in Proverbs 1:7, which states: "The fear of the Lord is the beginning of knowledge, but fools despise wisdom and discipline."

(Needed: Playing cards)

As kids arrive, give each a playing card. The cards will be used to divide into teams. Break into two or more teams, depending on the size of your group (two teams—black and red; three teams—numbers 2-5, 6-10, jack-ace; four teams—hearts, diamonds, clubs, spades; etc.). Have each team choose the wisest person in the group to compete in a "wisest group member" contest. Ask the teams to assemble as much proof of their candidates' wisdom as possible. After a few minutes, have each team present its candidate and explain why he or she is wisest. Ask an impartial panel of judges to vote on who's the wisest. Afterward, ask: **What is wisdom? What's the difference between being smart and being wise?**

DATE I USED THIS SESSION _____ GROUP I USED IT WITH _____

NOTES FOR NEXT TIME _____

_____

_____

1. What are some rules at your house? How do you feel about these rules? Which ones make sense? Which ones don't? What would life be like if there were no rules?

2. Read Proverbs 1:1-7. It's your job to write the back cover "blurb" for a new edition of Proverbs. The back cover "blurb" is the written description on the back of a book that's supposed to help someone who picks up the book decide to buy it. Knowing this, what would you write? (Group members might mention the author, what the book's about, what it's useful for, etc.)

3. Why do you think the fear of the Lord is the beginning of knowledge (1:7)? Why is it foolish to despise wisdom and discipline, according to Proverbs 1:7? (Note that fear involves a loving reverence for God and a willingness to trust Him. If this is our attitude, God can teach us many things. Many people would rather do as they please—these are the fools. It's easier to be foolish than wise.)

4. Proverbs 1:11 gives a graphic description of sinners "[lying] in wait for someone's blood"—trying to trap and victimize people by tempting them with various sins. What are some typical sins that entice and victimize today's teenagers? (These sins may involve any attempt to gain something that doesn't belong to you in the first place.)

5. Read Proverbs 1:20–4:27. **Make a list of the advantages of gaining wisdom and the consequences of not gaining wisdom.** (Advantages might include living in safety [1:33], finding the knowledge of God [2:5], protection [2:11], and long life [3:16]. Consequences might include destruction [1:32], death [2:18], sudden disaster [3:25], and shame [3:35].) **Which of these items make the most sense to you? Which don't seem to make sense?**

6. How do you go about finding the knowledge of God (2:5)? What are some specific things you can do to know God better? (Knowing God involves a lot more than knowing *things about* God [head knowledge]. It also involves knowing Him in personal experience [heart knowledge]. It means having a close, personal relationship with Him.)

7. How important is it to have a good name or reputation in life (3:4)? What's necessary to get a good reputation?

8. Rewrite Proverbs 3:5, 6 in language a four-year-old would better understand.

9. What do you think is the connection between your behavior and your health (3:2, 8, 16; 4:10, 22)? (Living in God's wisdom doesn't guarantee a longer life here on earth, but it does improve the odds—not to mention the value of an eternal life with God.)

10. Read all of the verses that have the words "my son" or "my sons" in them (1:8, 10, 15; 2:1; 3:1, 11, 21; 4:1, 10, 20). What is this parent trying to say? What do you imagine the child is about to do? Do you think the parent is too hyper? Why or why not? How do you feel when your parents give you advice? (Perhaps the child is leaving home. Perhaps the parent is very aware of the dangers "out there." The parent isn't trying to spoil the child's fun, but rather wants his son to enjoy life to its fullest.)

11. What might it cost you to get wisdom (4:7)? (Popularity, friends, time, etc.) What do you think would be some personal benefits to you as a result of becoming wise?

Distribute copies of the reproducible sheet, "Putting Words in their Mouths." Have half your group come up with wise words and half of your group come up with foolish words for each situation. Let kids work in groups of two or three to locate appropriate verses from Proverbs 1–4 for each situation. After a few minutes, ask group members to share what they wrote in the speech balloons and any verses they found to apply to these situations. Here's just one possibility from each chapter: Situation 1—Proverbs 1:10; Situation 2—Proverbs 2:12; Situation 3—Proverbs 3:29; Situation 4—Proverbs 4:13. Afterward, say: **Being wise has a lot more to do with what you do than with what you know. Do you agree or disagree with this statement?** (In many ways it's true—our behavior ultimately shows what we truly believe.)

Putting *Words* in Their *Mouths*

For each situation below, put some words in the speech balloons as directed by your fearless and wise leader. Then search through Proverbs 1–4 to find a verse or two that applies to each situation.

PROVERBS 5–9

Fool Proof

Having established the benefits of wisdom that come about only through fearing the Lord, the writer of Proverbs goes on to contrast wisdom and folly. Proverbs 5–7 contain several warnings against folly (foolishness); Proverbs 8 and 9 contrast the competing invitations of wisdom and folly.

Hand out copies of the reproducible sheet, "Fools Me!" Have kids write down a plausible explanation for each of the five questions. Write on one sheet the correct answers, which are as follows: (1) Two minutes earlier it was -4° F. This is the greatest temperature increase in the shortest time period on record; (2) The choice was decided by a coin toss; (3) They hold logs next to a fireplace; (4) It's a bag; (5) He used his first $105 Social Security check—he was 65 years old. After a few minutes, collect and shuffle the papers. For each question, read off five or six of the most plausible explanations (including the correct answer) and have kids guess (by number) which one is the real one. Award one point to those who correctly guess the real explanation and one point to those whose explanations were guessed to be real by other group members. Afterward, ask: **What's the difference between being fooled and being a fool? Today we're going to look at what Proverbs says about fools.**

DATE I USED THIS SESSION _____ GROUP I USED IT WITH _____

NOTES FOR NEXT TIME _____

_____

_____

1. Describe a time when you did something foolish. How did you feel about it then? How do you feel about it now?

2. Read Proverbs 5. **What can an unmarried person get out of these verses?** (The term "adulteress" could be taken to mean any person that's likely to lead you away from God. This could apply to friendships as well as dating relationships and certainly applies to keeping sexual relations within the confines of marriage.)

3. **What do you suppose it means to drink water from your own cistern** (5:15)? (Most agree that it applies to marriage—let your spouse alone satisfy your sexual desires. In a symbolic sense, it could be taken to mean seeking wisdom from God alone.) **Do you think the author of this stuff would say that sex is a dirty, shameful thing? Why or why not?** (Proverbs 5:17-19 suggests that in the context of marriage, sex is a beautiful, enjoyable blessing.)

4. Read Proverbs 6. **Sometimes hazardous things have warning labels attached to them. What are some of the hazardous things mentioned in these verses? What kind of warning labels might be attached to them?** (Some of the danger areas include promising something you can't deliver [6:1-5]; laziness [6:6-11]; insincerity [6:12-15]; pride, falsehood, troublemaking, etc. [6:16-19]; adultery [6:20-35].)

5. Read Proverbs 7. **Here's another warning against the adulteress. Why do you think the author is so concerned about adultery?** (Maybe he's very aware of the power of the sex drive on young people and the need to be wise about these things before temptations present themselves.)

6. **What would you say are the top three temptations that lead people your age down the wrong path today** (7:25-27)?

7. **What are some benefits of wisdom found in Proverbs 8?** (Understanding, sound judgment, riches and honor, life, and favor from the Lord.) **Who does wisdom remind you of in Proverbs 8:22-31?** (Jesus, who is the "wisdom of God." See I Corinthians 1:24 and Colossians 2:2, 3).

8. Read Proverbs 9. **How are wisdom and folly similar? How are they different?** (Both offer invitations to the "simple"—that is, those who lack judgment. Both have houses. Both offer some type of food or drink. Both call from the highest point of the city. Wisdom leads to understanding and life. Folly's ways lead to death. Wisdom actively seeks people out. Folly lazily sits around and entices people.)

9. **Give some examples of people today who follow after wisdom. Give some examples of people following folly.**

10. **Do wisdom's words in Proverbs 9:9-12 sound familiar? What are they saying?** (They are very similar to the words in Proverbs 1:5, 7. They summarize the message of Proverbs 1–9—that wisdom is valuable and only comes through a loving, reverent relationship with God. Any other way is foolishness and ultimately leads to destruction.)

11. **Based on Proverbs 5–9, how would you define a fool? What types of fools are described in this passage?** (Fools are those who reject God's wisdom. It's as if there are stages of foolishness—the simple just lack good judgment; mockers make fun of others; adulterers intentionally lead others astray; sluggards are lazy.)

Go back to Proverbs 6:16-19. List the seven things that are detestable to the Lord. Come up with some specific examples of each of these things and talk about why God hates them. Ask an artistic group member to draw the following on the board: eyes, tongue, hands, heart, and feet. Ask: **Which of these body parts is most likely to lead you into foolish behavior? For example, if you keep going places you know you shouldn't, maybe it's your feet. If you watch stuff on TV that you know you shouldn't, maybe it's your eyes.** Give other examples as needed. Have kids draw or write down the body part or parts that tend to get them in the most trouble. Allow for sharing as people are comfortable. Be willing to share something yourself to get the discussion started. Challenge kids to think of one specific thing they can do this week to seek wisdom rather than foolishness.

FOOLS ME!

Come up with a plausible-sounding explanation for each of the following questions. The object is to get others in the group to choose your explanation as being the truth. When you're done, dissect your paper along the dotted line, and turn in the top half.

1. At 7:32 A.M. on January 22, 1943, the temperature in Spearfish, South Dakota was 68° F. Why is this significant?

2. Why did Orville, and not Wilbur, Wright make the first manned flight at Kitty Hawk?

3. Sled dogs pull sleds. Sheepdogs guard sheep. What do firedogs do?

4. Ever heard the expression, "A pig in a poke"? What's a poke?

5. Where did Colonel Sanders, founder of Kentucky Fried Chicken, get the money he needed to start his fast food chain?

- ✂ -

ANSWERS

Guess which explanation is the real one.

1.

2.

3.

4.

5.

PROVERBS 10–31

Speaking Words of Wisdom

Having spent the first nine chapters setting up his premise that wisdom is superior to folly, the writer of Proverbs now includes a seemingly random collection of wise sayings. Most of these sayings are short, succinct thoughts, often contrasting one thing with another. The Book of Proverbs concludes with a description of the ideal wife, which is similar to the description of wisdom herself in chapters 1–9.

To begin the session, have kids form teams. Hand out paper and pencils. Instruct each team to write down as many wise sayings as possible in five minutes. (Examples might include "Early to bed, early to rise, makes a man healthy, wealthy, and wise"; "A stitch in time saves nine"; and "The early bird gets the worm.") Collect the sheets. The team that came up with the most sayings wins Round 1. For Round 2, you might play a game of charades, with contestants trying to get their teammates to guess wise sayings by acting them out. The team that correctly guesses the most sayings is the winner. Afterward, explain that in this session, you'll be looking at the most important collection of wise sayings ever written.

DATE I USED THIS SESSION _____ GROUP I USED IT WITH _____

NOTES FOR NEXT TIME _____

_____

_____

1. What are some sayings or expressions that people in your family use over and over? What's the best advice you've ever been given? (Famous sayings and expressions are sometimes easy to remember. They often contain some element of truth.)

2. Hand out copies of the reproducible sheet, "Treasure Hunt." Let kids work in small groups to search through Proverbs 10–31 to find suitable verses. You might want to divvy up the work, assigning certain chapters or certain areas listed on the sheet to each group. Allow about 10-15 minutes for searching; then have the groups share their discoveries. **What are some of your impressions of this book of the Bible now that you've dug through it a little? What interesting discoveries did you find?**

3. Read some proverbs dealing with one's relationship with God (10:27, 29; 14:2, 16, 27; 16:1-5, 9; 19:21, 23; 21:3). **What do these verses teach us about God? About those who fear God? About those who reject God?**

4. If the writer of Proverbs wrote a book on parent-child relationships, what do you think it might be called? What might some of the chapters deal with (10:1, 17; 11:29; 12:1; 13:1, 24; 15:5; 19:18, 20; 20:20; 23:13, 14, 22, 24; 29:15, 17)**?** (It would certainly focus a lot on discipline.) **Why is discipline so important?** (Without it, children don't learn what's appropriate. Note that the word "rod" [13:24; 23:13, 14; 29:15] doesn't necessarily mean something to spank with; it might refer to a shepherd's guiding rod.)

5. What advice does Proverbs contain for building solid friendships (12:26; 13:20; 17:17; 18:1, 24; 20:6; 22:24; 25:17; 27:5, 6, 9, 10, 17)**?** (It's important to choose friends wisely. A person can't have too many close friends. Some so-called "friends" can lead us in the wrong direction. True friends confront, even wound, one another.) **What's the difference between a companion and a true friend?**

6. Summarize what Proverbs is saying about "the tongue" in as few words as possible (10:8, 10, 11, 13, 19-21, 32; 15:1, 2, 4, 23; 16:23, 24, 28; 25:11, 15; 26:20-22, 28).

(Select your words carefully—they are very powerful both for good or for ill.) **Which verses do kids at your school most need to hear? Why?**

7. **According to Proverbs, what should your view of money and material possessions be** (11:4, 16, 24, 25, 26, 28; 13:7, 11; 14:21, 31; 15:16, 17; 19:17; 21:6, 13; 22:1, 9, 16; 23:4, 5; 28:22-27; 30:7-9)**?** (When life is over, money has no real value; therefore, it's to be shared with those who need it now. God rewards generosity. Money should be made honestly. Right living is much more important.) **Which verse do your parents most need to hear?**

8. **On one hand, Proverbs tells us not to wear ourselves out to get rich** (23:4)**; on the other hand, it says that hard work is good and makes one wealthy** (10:4, 5, 26; 12:11, 24; 13:4; 14:23; 18:9; 19:15; 24:30-34)**. What gives?** (There's more to work than making money. The focus should be on doing your best at work, not on getting wealthy.) **Give some examples of chasing fantasies** (12:11). (Lotteries, get-rich-quick schemes, etc.)

9. **What sense do you get that the writer(s) of Proverbs knew about the dangers of alcohol** (20:1; 23:20, 29-35; 31:4-7)**?** (Proverbs 23:29-35 paints a very vivid picture of what drunkenness is like.) **What do you think most people your age would say about these verses?**

(Needed: Art supplies)

We've looked at several verses today. Choose one verse that's especially meaningful to you right now. Share with someone else why it's meaningful. To help kids remember their verses, have them create a design for a billboard, bumper sticker, vanity plate, poster, or T-shirt that effectively captures the message of their proverb. Distribute paper and art supplies for kids to work with. After a few minutes, have them share their creations. Before closing in prayer, challenge group members to think of specific applications of their chosen proverbs in the coming week.

TREASURE HUNT

AAAARRRHH!!! THAR'S TREASURE IN THEM THAR PAGES! GRAB YER SHOVEL, MATEY, AND DIG THROUGH PROVERBS 10–31 TO SEE WHAT PRECIOUS GEMS YOU CAN DISCOVER IN EACH OF THE FOLLOWING AREAS.

PROVERBS

YOUR RELATIONSHIP WITH GOD.

YOUR RELATIONSHIP WITH YOUR PARENTS

YOUR USE OF YOUR TONGUE

YOUR RELATIONSHIP WITH FRIENDS

YOUR USE OF YOUR MONEY

YOUR USE OF YOUR TIME

YOUR USE OF ALCOHOLIC BEVERAGES

ECCLESIASTES 1–2; 4–6

Why Bother?

For the most part, the Book of Ecclesiastes presents a pessimistic view of life, stating that a life lived apart from God (under the sun) is utterly meaningless. The first few chapters support this thought over and over. The writer of Ecclesiastes believes that when life comes to its inevitable conclusion, wisdom, pleasures, work, advancement, and riches will mean absolutely nothing. Yet he is also convinced that God is indeed very real and that those things that have no meaning apart from God are, in fact, gifts from Him.

(Needed: Art supplies)

Bring in some art supplies with which your kids can create masterpieces. Explain that the masterpieces will all have the same title— "Under the Sun"—but that what group members create "under the sun" is up to them. After about five minutes or so, tell everyone to stop working. Gather the "masterpieces" and throw them away. Now that you have everyone's attention, launch into a reading of Ecclesiastes 1. If you have time, read or skim through the whole book, or at least enough to give group members a feel for it. As kids listen, have them sit down during any parts that sound depressing and stand up whenever they hear something hopeful or encouraging.

DATE I USED THIS SESSION _____ GROUP I USED IT WITH _____

NOTES FOR NEXT TIME _____

_____

_____

1. Who's the best teacher you've ever had? What made this teacher so good?

2. How would you like to study under the teacher who wrote Ecclesiastes 1? What would be the advantages and disadvantages of taking a class from this teacher?

3. Imagine that the teacher has just said everything is meaningless (1:2, 14) and asks if there are any questions. What would you ask? What arguments would you use to support or contradict what the teacher has just said? (It's important to know that the phrase "under the sun," which appears several times in the Book of Ecclesiastes, refers to a life lived apart from God. In that sense, everything is indeed meaningless.)

4. If wisdom brings sorrow, and knowledge brings grief, why bother with learning (1:18; 2:15)? (These do seem like strange words from the guy who wrote Proverbs. Again, knowledge sought apart from God has no eternal value.)

5. What are some empty pleasures that people today try to find meaning in, apart from God (2:1-11)? (Sports, hobbies, sex, etc.)

6. Why work (2:17-26)? (If a person sees work as a gift from God [2:24], then it can have real meaning and bring satisfaction. But if work is viewed apart from God, or "under the sun" [2:17, 18, 20, 22], then it is meaningless.) **Which view of work do you think most people hold? How about you?**

7. The words in Ecclesiastes 4:9-12 almost seem out of place among all of this depressing stuff. What point do you think the teacher is making? How have you seen these verses to be true? (If a person lives only for himself or herself, then his or her life is a waste. But if life is lived for the benefit of someone else, it has much more value. These words are often read at weddings, but they don't apply only to marriage.)

8. What application can you make from Ecclesiastes 5:1-7 about your behavior at church? (Go to church to listen and learn. Don't go there lightly or flippantly. Don't rush into making promises you won't be able to keep.)

9. What do you think the richest people in the country would say about Ecclesiastes 5:8–6:12? (Some wealthy people won't believe the truth in these verses. It's important to see that God gives us everything we own [5:19] and it's only through God that a person can enjoy these things. We know from elsewhere in Scripture that one of the surest ways to enjoy money and possessions is to share them with those in need.)

10. In Ecclesiastes 6:12, it sounds like the teacher doesn't know what happens after death. What would you tell him about it? (Again, we find those words "under the sun," suggesting that death apart from God is the ultimate in meaninglessness. The writer of Ecclesiastes lived before the full explanation of God's provision of eternal life in and through Christ.)

Hand out copies of the reproducible sheet, "What's the Use?" Instruct half of your group to give advice from the perspective of someone who lives "under the sun"—that is, someone who leaves God out of the picture. Instruct the other half to give advice from the perspective of someone who trusts in God. Let kids work in pairs, jotting down what they'd say to each individual seeking advice. After a while, go through each situation and let kids share the advice they'd give. Note the difference that trust in God makes in each case. Let group members share how God makes a difference in how they view life.

What's the Use?

What advice would you give to each of the following people?

Dear Mr./Ms. Advice:

I work really hard at school to get straight A's so that I'll be accepted to a good college. Trouble is, I've been studying so much that I don't have time for anything else. It seems like I have to work harder at school than other people I know. The stress is killing me. Sometimes I wonder if it's really worth it. What do you say?

Sincerely yours,

Afraid of B's in Cloverdale

Dear Mr./Ms. Advice:

I'm really lonely. I know a lot of people at school, but no one really knows me, if you know what I mean. I don't feel like I have any friends. I've tried church, but it's full of hypocrites. Part of my problem is that I know if I get really close to someone, I'll end up getting hurt. I see it happen all of the time. So, why bother?

Truly yours,

Longing in Long Island

Dear Mr./Ms. Advice:

I lay awake at night wondering what life is all about. What's the point, anyway? We grow up, go to school, get a job if we can find one, work for a few years, retire, and then die. Since we're all gonna die anyway, I sometimes think about getting it over with as soon as possible. Why shouldn't I?

Yours sincerely,

Sleepless in Seattle

Dear Mr./Ms. Advice:

I'm the original party animal. My motto in life is "Eat, drink, have sex, and be merry, for tomorrow you may die." I think that's even in the Bible somewhere. But sometimes I think there's got to be more to life than this. I need to drink more to get the same buzz; sometimes I worry about getting AIDS; and if I think about it long enough, I'm not that happy. What's wrong with me?

Yours truly,

Hungover in Hanover

ECCLESIASTES 3

What Time Is It?

In the middle of all of the talk about the meaninglessness of life sits Ecclesiastes 3, a beautiful passage about the nature of time in our lives. It says that there is a time for all sorts of things—some pleasant, some not so pleasant. It affirms that God is in control of all that happens and that He lives outside of time. He sets eternity in our hearts. The passage then questions whether people are any better off than animals, since they both end up returning to dust.

Get kids thinking about time with the reproducible sheet, "How Long Would It Take . . ." The sheet lists several activities and asks kids to guess how long each would take. Here are the answers: (1) 8.7 months; (2) 3.5 hours; (3) 2.6 days; (4) 5 minutes; (5) 15 hours; (6) 1.3 seconds; (7) 40 days (or 1.33 months); (8) 1 year; (9) 114 centuries; (10) 2.3 months; (11) 33 minutes; (12) 7 years; (13) 1 week; (14) 35.4 centuries; (15) 1.67 months (or 50 days); (16) 42.6 seconds; (17) 1 day; (18) 1.5 years (or 18 months); (19) 2.1 months; (20) 11 minutes. Spend some time talking about time. Ask: **What is time? What do people say about it? Some say "time flies when you're having fun." Some say "time seems to go faster the older you get." Do you agree? If so, does that mean older people have more fun than younger people?**

DATE I USED THIS SESSION _____ GROUP I USED IT WITH _____

NOTES FOR NEXT TIME _____

_____

_____

1. Describe the perfect day. What time would you wake up? What would your perfect day consist of? How much time would you spend doing each activity?

2. Read through Ecclesiastes 3. **What point do you think the teacher is trying to make?** (Maybe that we have little control over time, but God has complete control over it.)

3. Which of the items listed in Ecclesiastes 3:2-8 do you have control over? Which ones don't you have control over? What do people do to try to "control" time? (We certainly have no control over when we're born. We have some control over how long we live, but not ultimate control. We probably have little control over some of the events that might cause weeping and dancing.)

4. Go through each event listed in Ecclesiastes 3:2-8. When would be an appropriate time for each? (Scattering and gathering stones may refer to building or tearing down a house. It might also mean putting obstacles in an enemy's way or removing obstacles from your own way.)

5. What does Ecclesiastes 3:10, 11 mean? What burden has God laid on us? What is beautiful? What does it mean that God has set eternity in our hearts? Why can't we understand what God does? (These verses are crucial to understanding the passage. The burden God lays on us could be time itself. It might also refer to having to work for a living. Yet all of God's gifts, including the gifts of time and work, are beautiful and to be enjoyed. But because we were created in His image and have eternity in our hearts, deep down we realize that there has to be more to life than what happens during our time on earth. Even so, we can't really see time from God's perspective. We can never fully understand why things happen the way they do.)

6. What are some things about God that you don't understand (3:11)? What are some things about God that you're sure of (3:14)?

7. Some people think time is theirs to spend any way they please. What does Ecclesiastes 3:17 say about that

notion? (What we do with our time matters to God. Someday He'll "judge" us all [the righteous and the wicked] for how we spent our time.)

8. **How do you feel about the judging side of God's character?** (It's consistent with His love and holiness. He can't tolerate injustice and wickedness; these things can't go unpunished. Thankfully for us, God has taken steps through the sacrifice of Jesus Christ to spare us the punishment we deserve for our sins if we trust in Him.)

9. **The teacher implies that people are no different from animals** (3:18-21). **Do you agree or disagree? Why?** (We're equal in the sense that we all die. If there's no afterlife, then logic would suggest that there really is no difference. Fortunately, God has bigger plans for us than our lives on this earth. If we lose sight of that, we can feel awfully insignificant.)

10. **How would you answer the question posed at the end of Ecclesiastes 3:22, which asks, Who can bring us to see what happens after we die?** (Only God can. Remember that this was written before Christ came to earth. Now that Jesus has come, He has revealed much more about our eternal destiny. See II Timothy 1:9, 10.)

Have someone read Ecclesiastes 3:11. Discuss what it means to have eternity set in our hearts. Do all of your group members really believe this? Look up John 17:3 for a glimpse of what eternal life is all about. It's much more than living forever—it involves knowing Jesus personally and intimately. Challenge group members who have kept Jesus at arm's length to seek to know Him better. Then look at the second half of Ecclesiastes 3:11. Ask why people try to figure God out. In many ways, the more we get to know Him, the more mysterious He becomes. However, it's also true that the more we know Him, the more we are able to trust Him. Spend some time praising God for who He is and for what He's done for us through Christ.

HOW LONG WOULD IT TAKE...

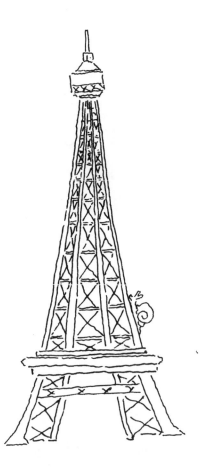

1. To swim (non-stop) around the equator?

2. For a sound wave to travel from Los Angeles to New York?

3. For a snail to climb the Eiffel Tower?

4. To count all of the beans in an eight-ounce can of baked beans?

5. To pull out every hair on the average human's head (one at a time)?

6. For light to travel from the earth to the moon?

7. To count every letter in the Bible?

8. For lightning to strike the earth two billion times?

9. To read (at a rate of 300 words per minute) all of the books in the Library of Congress?

10. To write the first and last names of one million people?

11. For light to travel from Earth to Jupiter?

12. For the average human body to replace every cell?

13. For a full-grown oak tree to expel 49 tons of water through its leaves?

14. To walk to the sun?

15. For the average human to consume his or her weight in food?

16. For a penny to fall from the height of Mount Everest to the ground?

17. For the human heart to pump 13,000 quarts of blood?

18. For a newly minted U.S. dollar bill to be taken out of circulation?

19. To hike across the U.S. and back again?

20. For a two-and-one-half-inch birthday candle to burn itself out?

Without using a calculator, decide if the time it would take to do each of the above would be seconds, minutes, hours, days, weeks, months, years, decades, or centuries. Don't take all day figuring this out—just guess. Extra credit: How many seconds, minutes, hours, days, weeks, months, years, decades, or centuries would each take?

ECCLESIASTES 11–12

Time Is on Your Side

Chapters 7–11 of Ecclesiastes continue with many of the same themes introduced in the first six chapters: the meaninglessness of life lived apart from God, the fact that all people eventually die, and the seeming randomness of life. The book concludes with a call to young people to enjoy the days of their youth because old age is no picnic. After thinking about growing old, the teacher again calls everything meaningless. But the book doesn't end there. It goes on to say that the most important thing in life is to fear God and keep His commandments, and that only then does life have any lasting meaning.

(Needed: Guest speakers [optional])

If possible, invite some older members of your congregation to join your group. Begin with a question-and-answer session about what it's like to grow old. What advice would these seniors give to your kids? If it's not possible to get guest speakers for your meeting, try another activity. Have kids form groups. Let each group create a top ten list of things that happen to you when you get old. Allow for humor, but remind kids to show respect for older people. Afterward, ask: **Why do some people dread getting old? What do you think is the best thing about getting old? What's the worst thing?**

DATE I USED THIS SESSION _____ GROUP I USED IT WITH _____

NOTES FOR NEXT TIME _____

_____

_____

1. **What do you expect to be doing fifty years from now?** (It's hard for young people to think that far ahead, but help them see that fifty years is just a "drop in the bucket" in the scope of all time.)

2. **In Ecclesiastes 11:7–12:1, the teacher gives a lot of advice to the young people he's teaching. Put each piece of advice into your own words.** (Enjoy all of your days, especially when you're young, because you have fewer hardships now. Don't ignore the fact that you're going to grow older. Follow your dreams, but don't leave God out of the picture. Don't worry about the future—enjoy life to its fullest while you can. Don't forget about God, even when you're young and may not feel much need for Him.)

3. **What images or pictures of old age are found in Ecclesiastes 12:2-5?** (Failing eyesight; poor teeth; creaking or aching joints; loss of hearing; increased fear of harm; white hair [12:5]; loss of energy; loss of desire, possibly referring to sexual desire; death itself.)

4. **How does Ecclesiastes 12:6, 7 describe death? What other images might you use?**

5. **What do you think most people your age think and feel about growing old and dying? How do you feel about it? What worries you most when you think about growing old? What do you most look forward to about growing older?**

6. **What do people do to try to prolong their youth? Why are so many people fearful of old age and death?**

7. **Does Ecclesiastes 12:8 sound familiar? Where have you heard it before?** (It's how the book started—see Ecclesiastes 1:2. It's one of the main conclusions of the book. Without God, life is meaningless.)

8. **Some people think Ecclesiastes has no place in the Bible. What do you think** (12:9-11)**?** (These words are from a very wise teacher. They're hard words that a lot of people don't want to think about. Some people think the Christian life should be all sunshine and smiles, and think this book is too depressing. They're missing the point. Ecclesiastes 12:11 implies that these words come from the Lord, the Great Shepherd, Himself.)

9. **Who do you think most needs to memorize the second part of Ecclesiastes 12:12, which states that the process of making books never ends and that too much studying wearies the body?** (Possibly students, teachers, or even publishing company executives!)

10. **Summarize the conclusion of the Book of Ecclesiastes** (12:13, 14). **Do you agree with it? Why or why not? How do these words make you feel?** (The only way to find meaning in life is to live for God. Some might be frightened of His judgment. But if we trust in Him, there's no need to fear.)

11. **So, when it's all said and done, is life meaningless or meaningful?** (It depends on your perspective and whether or not you have entered into a trusting relationship with God.)

The reproducible sheet, "Jumping to Conclusions," will help summarize the main message of the Book of Ecclesiastes. Let kids work on the sheet individually. After a few minutes, give them an opportunity to share some of the things they've written. Emphasize that fearing God means much more than being afraid of Him—it involves a loving respect for who He is. This type of fear should draw us closer to Him, not drive us away. Discuss the relationship between fearing God and obeying Him. Note that the reverence of God comes first. Once we experience His love, our natural response is one of wanting to obey Him. The Christian life is more than following a bunch of rules. The rules only make sense in the context of a loving relationship with God. As you close the session in prayer, let group members read the prayers they've written ("God, right now I'm feeling . . ."). To break the ice, you should read what you've written first. Be available to talk privately with kids who want to get more serious about their relationship with God.

JUMPING TO CONCLUSIONS

Now all has been heard;
   here is the conclusion of the matter:
Fear God and keep his commandments,
   for this is the whole duty of man.
For God will bring every deed into judgment,
   including every hidden thing, whether it is
   good or evil.

Ecclesiastes 12:13, 14

What does it mean for you to fear God?

What commandments do you have a particularly hard time with?

Why should you keep God's commandments?

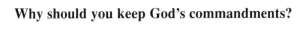

What are some of the "good" hidden things in your life?

What are some of the "evil" hidden things in your life?

How would you complete the following prayer?

God, right now I'm feeling . . .

SONG OF SONGS

Just Another Silly Love Song?

According to I Kings 4:32, Solomon wrote 1,005 songs. This is the greatest of them all—thus, its title, the Song of Songs. Full of imagery and symbolism, it's a celebration of love between two lovers, with occasional commentary from the beloved's friends. It affirms both the beauty and power of love.

As group members arrive, have them call out various words to complete the mad lib on the reproducible sheet, "Love Letters." The structure for the letters is taken straight from Song of Songs. The letter written by the male is from Song of Songs 4:1-4. (We thought it best to stop before verse 5.) The letter written by the female is from Song of Songs 5:10-16. Have some fun with this activity. After the words are filled in, explain that you've just discovered two love letters. You might want to have the "author" of each letter actually read it aloud—without laughing. Afterward, explain that you'll be looking at what the lovers really said in Song of Songs.

DATE I USED THIS SESSION _____ GROUP I USED IT WITH _____

NOTES FOR NEXT TIME _____

_____

_____

1. What's one of your favorite songs on the radio right now? Why do you like it? What station plays the best love songs? What's the best love song ever written?

2. Read through the entire Song of Songs. **If this song were set to music, what style of music might be most appropriate? What artist or group would do the best job of recording it? What age group should the song be targeted at? What sections would make the best lyrics? What sections would and wouldn't be sung during a church service?**

3. There are many aspects to love—physical, emotional, and spiritual. **What percent of Song of Songs would you say focuses on the physical aspects of love? What percent focuses on the emotional aspects? What percent focuses on the spiritual aspects?** (The book focuses primarily on the physical, with references to kisses, embraces, physical appearance, etc.) **Why do you think this song speaks so much about physical things?** (In the early stages of romantic love, that's often one of the main things on lovers' minds. But that's not to say that the emotional and spiritual aspects of the relationship aren't also very important.)

4. What indications are there that the lovers are married? (Song of Songs 3:11 suggests an earlier wedding.)

5. What references to nature are included in this song? Why are there so many? What do they mean? (References include doves, does, gazelles, vineyards, gardens, lilies, fawns, etc. Most of the references are symbolic of something physical or sexual.) What are some of the references that seem odd today? How might we rephrase these references using modern language? (We might describe teeth as being like pearls instead of like shorn sheep.)

6. The phrase, "Do not arouse or awaken love until it so desires," is mentioned three times (2:7; 3:5; 8:4). What does it mean? How do you keep from awakening it? (All three times, the phrase follows some expression of physical or sexual intimacy. This suggests that once sexual passion is aroused, it's pretty hard to keep it in check. Therefore, it shouldn't be awakened until after marriage.)

7. What season is the setting for this song (2:11; 7:12)? Why is spring often associated with romantic love? Why are sexual feelings usually stronger at night (3:1; 5:2)?

8. Song of Songs 2:16; 6:3; and 7:10 say that lovers belong to one another. In what sense is that true? When does possessiveness become detrimental or dangerous to a relationship? (When it becomes one-sided; when it excludes concern for others.)

9. Read Song of Songs 8:6, 7. What does it mean to place someone as a seal over your heart? (A seal indicates a sign of lasting commitment.) What kinds of "seals" do people use today? (Rings, vows, tattoos, bracelets, necklaces, etc.)

10. How powerful is love? Give some examples. Song of Songs 8:6, 7 makes it sound like jealousy is OK. Is it? (There can be positive jealousy—similar to God being jealous [Exodus 20:5] when people seek after other things.)

11. If love is so strong and so hard to quench, why are so many marriages in shambles and why is the divorce rate so high? (Maybe the commitments are shallow to begin with. Maybe the couples have unreal expectations of how love changes with time.)

Song of Songs deals with the early, romantic stages of a relationship when couples are head over heels in love—that is, infatuated with one another. In many ways, it seems to describe the honeymoon period. For a relationship to last, it has to be based on much more than physical attraction. Make a list of the components of an ideal, long-lasting guy-girl relationship. Have kids rank the items in terms of their overall importance. Then make a list of the biggest things that threaten a healthy guy-girl relationship. Again, let individuals rank the items on the list. Talk about things your kids can be doing right now to prepare for long-term, healthy dating and marriage relationships. Close with a prayer celebrating the beautiful gift of love God has given us and affirming the wonder of sexual intimacy within the marriage relationship.

Love Letters

Dearest _____,
(name of a female group member)

How _____ you are, my _____, how _____! Your eyes
(adjective)   (term of endearment)   (adjective)

behind your _____ are _____. Your hair is like a flock
(something worn on the head)   (type of bird [plural])

of _____ descending from _____. Your teeth are like a
(type of animal [plural])   (something really tall)

flock of _____ just _____, coming up from
(type of animal [plural])   (something that happens to animals)

the _____.... Your lips are like a _____ _____; your
(verb ending in -ing)   (a color)   (clothing accessory)

mouth is _____. Your temples behind your _____ are like
(adjective)   (something worn on the head)

the halves of a _____. Your neck is like the _____ built with
(type of fruit)   (a tall structure)

_____; on it hang _____ _____.
(noun)   (a number)   (noun [plural])

Love forever, _____
(name of a male group member)

Dearest _____,
(name of a male group member)

You are _____ and _____, outstanding among _____.
(adjective)   (adjective)   (a number)

Your head is _____ _____; your hair is _____
(adjective)   (a color)   (adjective)

and _____ as a _____. Your eyes are like _____
(a color)   (type of bird)   (type of bird [plural])

by the _____, washed in _____, mounted like
(something found on a map)   (something people drink)

_____.... Your arms are like rods of _____.
(something people wear)   (something objects are made out of)

Your body is like polished _____, decorated with _____....
(brand of soap)   (type of decoration)

Your mouth is _____, itself; you are altogether _____.
(noun ending in -ness)   (adjective)

Love forever, _____
(name of a female group member)